D0378544

HOMESTEAD

Homestead

A N N I C K   S M I T H

MILKWEED

EDITIONS

Published 1995 by Milkweed Editions
Printed in the United States of America
Jacket design by Adrian Morgan / Red Letter
Cover photo by Stephen Simpson / FPG International: Paradise Valley, Montana
Endsheet photo by Randy Balsmeyer
Art for *Literature for a Land Ethic* by Betsy Bowen
The detail at the beginning of each essay is a dovetail joint from Annick Smith's home.
Book design by Will Powers. The text of this book is set in Granjon.

96 97 98 99 00   5 4 3 2 1

First Edition

Milkweed Editions is a not-for-profit publisher. We gratefully acknowledge support
from the Dayton Hudson Foundation for Dayton's and Target Stores; Ecolab
Foundation; General Mills Foundation; Honeywell Foundation; Jerome Foundation;
John S. and James L. Knight Foundation; The McKnight Foundation; Andrew
W. Mellon Foundation; Minnesota State Arts Board through an appropriation by the
Minnesota State Legislature; Musser Fund; Challenge and Literature Programs of
the National Endowment for the Arts; I. A. O'Shaughnessy Foundation; Piper
Family Fund of the Minneapolis Foundation; Piper Jaffray Companies, Inc.;
John and Beverly Rollwagen Fund of the Minneapolis Foundation; The St. Paul
Companies, Inc.; Star Tribune/Cowles Media Foundation; Surdna Foundation;
James R. Thorpe Foundation; Unity Avenue Foundation; Lila Wallace-Reader's
Digest Literary Publishers Marketing Development Program, funded through a
grant to the Council of Literary Magazines and Presses; and generous individuals.

Library of Congress Cataloging-in-Publication Data

Smith, Annick, 1936–.
    Homestead / Annick Smith. – 1st ed.
      p. cm.
    ISBN 1-57131-206-4 (cloth)
    ISBN 1-57131-213-7 (paper)
    1. Montana—Description and travel   2. Montana—Social life and customs.
    3. Smith, Annick, 1936– —Homes and haunts—Montana. I. Title.
F735.S65 1995
978.6–dc20   94–40312
                                                   CIP

For my family:
Helene, Steve, Kathy, Carole,
Eric, Stephen, Alex, Andrew, and Bill

And in memory of David Smith

Homestead

Acknowledgments

Thanks mostly to Bill Kittredge, who said I could write and showed me how. Also to the ones who are gone, Dave Smith and Dick Hugo, who inspired me and taught me to fight against the odds. I thank the Rattlesnake Ladies Salon — Dee McNamer, Kate Gadbow, Marnie Prange, Connie Poten, Jocelyn Siler, Sharon Barrett, Patricia Goedicke — who listened and critiqued. I also thank the editorial board of *The Last Best Place,* who educated me in the literature of the West: Mary Clearman Blew, Jim Welch, Bill Bevis, Bill Lang, Rich Roeder. And Ivan and Carol Doig, who urged me to write a memoir. And Terry Tempest Williams, who suggested this book while we rafted the Grand Canyon, then helped put the pieces together. I am grateful for the encouragement of Mark Bryant and Laura Hohnhold at *Outside* magazine, who kept me going by publishing my personal essays. And finally I thank Emilie Buchwald, a gentle editor who made me work harder than I thought I should, but who knows best.

HOMESTEAD

Homestead

The weathered log buildings on a hillside with yellow
grass would own me. From my first sight of the place, I
was hooked. I started to invent a new life. Some country
family lived in the mud-chinked house with sun glinting
off its tin roof, but the ranch seemed abandoned, no sounds
except the humming of yellow jackets, dry grass rustling as
we passed. A few leghorns pecked at the last grasshoppers
of summer. Home. If I lived here, who would I be?

I imagined a sturdy woman with skin lined and
cracked as the hewn logs. She would be chopping kindling
on the hard-packed dirt outside the kitchen door. Her man
drove a John Deere tractor along ditch banks thick with
sedge, timothy, and high, green tufts of orchard grass. Her
horseback children raced across the upper meadows. My
husband was a college professor; I was a city-bred wife.
Could this ever be our family?

In their youth, like so many other pilgrim artists,
my Jewish parents had left Hungary for the culture of exile
in 1920s Paris. At the apex of the Great Depression, before
Hitler and his collaborators claimed most of Europe,
they took the boat for the United States and settled in
Chicago. I grew up without an extended family, for most
of my great-aunts, uncles, and cousins—those who stuck to

the homeland—had disappeared. Some ended in the ovens of Auschwitz, others escaped to who knows where.

Mobility was the lesson: do not tie yourself to one place. Montparnasse is where I was born; Chicago was the dwelling of my childhood; and after I married David Smith at nineteen, we lived in Seattle for six years, until he was offered a job teaching English at the University of Montana.

In 1964, when Dave and I came to Missoula with our first two boys, friends in Seattle made bets about how long we would stay. They were not betting against Dave. He had grown up in a small Minnesota town and liked to fish and hunt and keep to himself. But me? I went to concerts and art shows and walked in Chinatown. I shopped for teas, rice wine, and spices whose names I could not pronounce. Home was streets full of strangers, green leafy vegetables thrown away into the rain-filled gutters. The chickens for sale in fly-blown markets were alive and squawking.

"Montana?" said one friend. "I give you a year. Maybe two." In our private mythology I was the grasshopper, and everyone knows a grasshopper will never turn into an ant. Thirty years later David is dead, all four boys are grown and gone away from Missoula, and I'm still living outback in Montana. I am that woman chopping her wood.

The day I first saw our home place, a sign at the cattle guard read "County road maintenance ends here." I have added my own sign in day-glow scarlet, "No hunting or trespassing." Sometimes I lock the gate so no one can drive onto the quarter mile of dirt road that leads to my house. It's not that I despise people; I simply love to weed my garden in solitude. Sometimes I think I am attached to my ground like the ghosts of its Swedish settlers. Sometimes I

feel rooted as the western larch and ponderosa pine. I think
everything that has ever lived here inhabits the place, even
the migrating birds: kestrels, snipe, bluebirds, red-tail
hawks. I think the place inhabits me.

Elk on new grass in May are part of the life I have
chosen, and a yellow, brittle day in August when a honey-
colored bear cub lies belly-up in a thorn-apple thicket,
heedlessly stripping ripe berries as I yank knapweed from
the roadside maybe thirty yards upwind. A coyote bitch
and two pups den in the culvert under the road. From our
log house on the meadow, I study the coyotes through
binoculars. Their ears are tipped fox red. No two days are
the same, no season returns, and I am never bored with the
stories I find in this land. I live in my city.

□   □   □

Since I was a girl, I have had a recurring vision of a house,
so vivid I thought for years it was actual. The house in my
dream is Victorian, with gabled roofs and a tower. The roof
is tiled in red clay, warm and Spanish, substantial and
abstract as a Cezanne. Sometimes the roof is blue. Always
there are chimneys. Many chimneys.

The upper stories are sided in white-painted cedar
shingles weathered to where the wood shows through. The
house sits on high ground. I cannot remember ever dreaming it in a valley. It has stood for generations surrounded by
gardens of poppies, blue-eyed cornflowers, flashing white
daisies, and climbing roses. There is a hedge of heavy-
scented purple lilac and the sounds of winged insects. A
few tall oaks or maples shade the house in cool green
refracted light.

I often come upon this place on a walk, see it rise out of mist in a soft Northwest Coast rain. I am never there in the night or in snow, although I love winter. Sunset is possible. The house exists in pastoral separateness. Not on a farm. Not in the city. There are no animals, except a shepherd dog who sometimes walks by my side. I've had three such dogs.

The entrance and main rooms are built of rocks glowing amber and aquamarine, like river stones under running water. There are spacious rooms paneled in mahogany, and a maroon velvet window seat where I can curl up and look through leaded glass windows. The birds are outside and cannot get in — ruby-throated hummingbirds, large and silent as bats. I flinch from the beat of their emerald wings.

Stairways surprise me. I find them where I least expect, always with delight, and explore where they lead. My bedroom is the tower.

There might be people — my mother and father, old friends from school, my little-girl sisters, my grandmother speaking Hungarian, a baby son. David, the fair boy I married before either of us had grown up, is usually with me or in another room. Perhaps I am making this up out of memories rather than dreams. The people are vague. What I remember so clearly is the house.

◲　◲　◲

Dave and I wanted to build our own house in Montana. We studied plans for packaged cedar houses and drew blueprints for a remodeled hip-roofed barn with a study and bedroom in the hayloft. Our most elaborate fantasy was inspired by a mine shaft near the ghost town of Garnet, three levels stepping down a slope to the creek. We photographed the site from every angle and measured the dimensions. At the top of the shaft we would build an octagonal, book-lined gazebo with views all around. Terraced walkways with solar panels and greenhouse orange trees would connect one level to the next. A great plan for millionaires.

We had started our search for land to build on in the Bitterroot Valley, the once-paradise of western Montana where Flathead Indians had lived amid an abundance of deer, elk, ducks, and geese. The Bitterroot River ran with native cutthroat trout, and its meadows flowered pink with bitterroot in spring, then blue and purple with lupine and camas. We almost bought fourteen acres of swamp on the Bitterroot River at the mouth of Lolo Creek, where Lewis and Clark had made their camp. They named it Traveler's Rest.

(Lewis) July 3, 1806. *The mosquitoes were so excessively troublesome this evening that we were obliged to kindle large fires for our horses. These insects torture them in such manner until they placed themselves in the smoke of the fires, that I really thought they would become frantic.*

Mosquitoes were not in our plans. Neither were swamps, no matter how filled with history. We were looking for open land cut by a river loaded with trout, or bordering a stream or a lake. It had to be within a half hour of the university in Missoula, where Dave taught courses in Victorian literature and the romantic poets. Finding nothing suitable in the Bitterroot, we expanded our search to the Clark Fork Valley from Clinton to Alberton, and up on the Salish/Kootenai Reservation beyond Evaro Hill.

Dave wanted space and silence. "I want to be backed up against wilderness," he said. "No neighbors I can see. Nothing."

He had his reasons. Dave was thirty-seven and I was thirty-four. We were young, and already life seemed to be closing down on us. An athlete since childhood, a high school star who went to college on a basketball ride, Dave couldn't walk fast without losing his breath. He was afraid to pick up our hefty three-year-old twins.

For two years we had known David was suffering an incurable and hereditary metabolic disorder. Cholesterol that his body could not process clogged his coronary arteries nearly to closure, despite blood-thinning drugs. Twice he had been rushed to the intensive care ward of St. Patrick's Hospital, and when we decided to buy land, he had recently returned from the University of Washington Medical Center in Seattle, where specialists had ruled out a bypass operation.

"It's not advisable in your case," is what the doctors told him. What they did not tell us was the damage was beyond repair. Researchers had not yet developed the minuscule balloons you can insert into clogged arteries to clear them out, or laser surgery to burn away the fatty deposits. The cholesterol-lowering drug for which Dave had been a guinea pig might help save our boys, but it could not save him. Dave was suffering a disease of the heart that we knew would lead inevitably to his premature death.

Death was coming, but we did not know where or when, and we looked for solace in nature undisturbed. With our four boys we hoped to escape into space and silence and privacy. We would go away into the illusion that time could not touch us.

"I want to listen to the moon rise." David yearned for the comfort of old, slow cycles. Indian moons and harvests and the minute changes of a season as it turns.

ɕ   ɕ   ɕ

Our realtor, having exhausted all prospects in three valleys, offered his hole card. "There's twenty acres on a year-round stream called Bear Creek," he said. "Some of the best trout fishing you'll ever see. You boys like to hunt?" The two older boys, Eric, who was fourteen, and Steve, twelve, nodded although they had never hunted anything larger than a duck. "White-tails and elk," he said. "I'm telling you, the hunting's out of sight."

This particular Bear Creek (there are hundreds of them in Montana) flows into the Big Blackfoot River some twenty miles northeast of Missoula. It is snow-belt country, high and cold, and you must travel to it on Highway 200, an icy asphalt ribbon that winds through the canyon of the Blackfoot until the land opens from lichen-encrusted rock cliffs to what is called Camas Prairie. Bad roads and worse weather had protected this area from the commuter subdivisions of the milder Bitterroot. In the fall of 1970 good land was still available, still cheap. The realtor turned right at Bear Creek Road, over a culvert where Union Creek widens to form a small pond. I had no idea that for years to come I would be watching for muskrats in that pond.

The pond would be our bus stop. We'd be bundled in our Land Rover, waiting for the 7:30 A.M. school bus to take Eric and Steve twenty miles to the high school in Missoula, and then the 8:00 bus that would carry the twins,

Alex and Andrew, five miles up the road to the three-room
school at Potomac. As dawn lighted far-off peaks of the
Bob Marshall Wilderness to the east, the black pond turned
silver, then salmon pink. The boys and I observed a resident beaver until he moved upstream; once a black bear
sow bathed with her cubs. When it was Dave's turn to
drive the kids to the highway, he brought Kipling's *Just-So
Stories* and read aloud "The Cat Who Walks by Itself." The
heater hummed in the Land Rover, he inhaled the musk of
little-boy bodies, and their breathing coated the windows
with steam.

But on that fall day in 1970 I paid no attention to the
pond. I looked around me at the fertile Blackfoot Valley,
where fields of oats and alfalfa were scattered among hay
pastures. I saw grazing cattle, a few modest houses, and
double-wide trailers where loggers lived. We drove three
miles up the gravel track bordered by pine forest and
turned right at Bear Creek Ranch.

Jack pines abruptly opened to highland meadows
burnt by early frosts and dotted with scarlet-leafed bushes
whose names I did not know. Later I would become familiar with the special flavors and culinary uses of each species:
the blue, mealy serviceberry, which is fine to pick and nib-
ble as you walk; the thorn apple, which is best left for birds
and bears; and the chokecherry, whose small, dark fruit
makes a pungent, wine-red jam and syrup for your pancakes.

Timbered hills rose to the south and west, clear-cuts
pocketing the ridges, and beyond stood unassuming Mt.
Olson, dusted with September snow. I got out of the rig to
open the gate. "Forest Service?" I asked, eyeing the scarred
forest. "Private industrial forest," said the realtor. "From

here to Bonner and over the top to Clinton. Like you wanted," he said. "This is the end of the public road."

I hated those clear-cuts, but the woods around them were dark with tall pine and streaked with western larch beginning their turn to sun yellow. The meadows tipped downward, emptying due north into the Big Blackfoot River. Across the river at the northern horizon, hills rose above Gold Creek to the distant Rattlesnake Mountains.

Before driving any further, we stopped to regard the view. Ranch buildings clustered on the western slope of the adjoining property, etched in flat autumn light. The old homestead was dominated by a great log barn with a high-pitched silvery shake roof and a wide-mouthed loft. Next to the barn was an outsized cement-block garage, a tall narrow granary, a pigpen, and a shed. The long, low, hewn-log ranch house stood across from the barn, and beyond it were a log bunkhouse, a henhouse, a small cabin, and a red-painted frame structure. Except for the barn, all the buildings were roofed in tin. They shone like mirrors in the bright afternoon.

In hay meadows above the compound a couple dozen white-faced Herefords grazed alongside their fat spring calves. Huge rock piles rose like hillocks above the tall grass. "Holy shit," said the realtor. "Some poor son of a bitch picked every damned one of those rocks by hand."

The rock piles were monuments, all right, to the hard-handed Swedes who homesteaded the place in 1882. It was a parklike virgin forest a century ago, with a few natural springs surrounded by great ponderosas and grassy meadows. Christborgs and Petersens had cleared the land with cross-cut saws, pulled stumps with teams of work-horses or mules, and built the log house and the barn. They pried rocks from the heavy clay soil and hauled them on stoneboats so they could till the fields for barley and oats.

After World War I, the Swedes sold out to a clan of Yugoslavs. The new immigrants completed an elaborate gravity-flow irrigation system with ditches and a wooden flume that channeled water from Bear Creek over two miles of shale mountainsides to empty at the top of the meadow. They fenced and watered the hundred acres of cleared land into a perfection of farming that made their homestead a showpiece. Yankee ranchers in the valley would come to marvel at its green grainfields when their own bottomland pastures were stunted and starved. All this I discovered in time, starting with the history embedded in the title to the land. But that first day I felt caught with wonder, a sense of recognition from a part of my being I did not know. Here, so unexpected, was home. Not the Victorian house of my dreams, but a homestead I could live on. It belonged to someone else. I never thought it could be ours.

The twenty acres of creek land the realtor had brought me to see was impossible. Too narrow, too damp, too dark in the depths of Bear Creek Canyon, weedy. Leaving, I made the realtor stop again at the top of the hill. "This," I said, pointing to the homestead. Could he find us such a place? What would it cost?

"Wait a minute," he said. I imagined his mind flipping through a catalog of Polaroids: dim, boxy houses with daylight basements; modern ranchettes and prefab houses; treeless subdivision lots—one artless image after another. The realtor frowned. "I think that place there, that one hundred sixty, the Vannoy place. It might be for sale."

And it was. One hundred and sixty-three acres. A

section of land is 640 acres; a quarter-section is 160 acres; we would receive an extra three acres to adjust for the curvature of the earth. It's a good uneven number. Nature will not conform to right-angles or triangles or circles marked with a surveyor's transit. Adjusted to the curvature of the earth was just fine. For $56,000 the whole shebang could be ours.

◪ ◪ ◪

Subsistence homesteading has never been easy in Montana. The climate is too harsh, the land too poor. After World War II it became a loser's game. Walter and Clara Vannoy knew that. Since 1949, when they bought the place from the Yugoslavs, the Vannoys had struggled to make a living off a starvation outfit. They raised eight children in the one-and-a-half-story ranch house. Clara and the kids tended to the stock, the hay, and the garden, while Walter tried to keep the large family solvent by hiring out as a gyppo logger and hauling cattle in his truck-and-trailer livestock rig.

I wonder what the Vannoys thought when Dave and I knocked on their door, eager to buy their land. It was the era of the *Whole Earth Catalog*, and log houses had become fashionable among intellectuals searching for authenticity. True country people saw log shacks as crude and uncivilized. If you could afford the materials, you would cover your logs with aluminum siding. The Vannoys had covered their walls with Sheetrock, which offered insulation and respectability. They had hidden their worn plank floors under linoleum in the kitchen, blue shag carpet in the living room. The low-eaved upper story had served as a dormitory bedroom for their kids. We knew at once we would tear off the Sheetrock.

With most of their children grown and gone off, the Vannoys wanted out. They had bought new pasture for their cattle and horses twenty miles east on the Clearwater River, near a truck-stop restaurant they wanted to lease. Clara hoped to make a better living serving coffee and home-baked apple pie to fishermen, hunters, and the salesmen passing on their mountain route between Great Falls and Missoula. Our down payment would help build them a modern house, our monthly payments would be a twenty-year insurance policy against failure. We closed the deal in December of 1970—the best Christmas present ever—and began the work of building a hideout.

Fear had transfixed Dave ever since he discovered his heart disease. For three years, the rest of us lived under his cloud. But as we prepared to move to our new home, his depression lifted. Each day of manual labor on the ranch gave Dave new strength, even though he knew overexertion could bring on a fatal attack. Dave put worry out the window. He stopped calling his cardiologist at each new twinge of angina, laid off on his blood-thinning medicines, and filled his mind with plans for improving things. Each weekend, and whenever else we could manage, David and I and our carpenter/writer friend, Jon Jackson, arrived at the homestead with tools and lumber. We were transforming the Vannoy's red-painted shack, built to shelter Christmas-tree harvesters, into a study. We wanted a quiet, private room to work in, a library for our books.

On the last Sunday of January, as a Chinook rainstorm pelted down on three feet of snow, the Blackfoot country became a sheet of glare ice with snow-melt rivers running over it. Going up to work on the homestead, Dave and Jon and I, along with our four boys, got stuck without chains on the steepest grade of Bear Creek Road. We carried our tools to the ranch.

Walter and Clara had fed the stock and were pulling out in their pickup as we arrived. We sloshed past the ranch house to the red shack and went to work painting new bookshelves that rose from floor to ceiling. When dusk came, we trooped downhill to visit our new neighbors on the creek, and they warmed us with hot chocolate, gave us a ride in their chained-up Toyota 4x4, and pulled our car out of the ditch. Gliding back to Missoula over black ice, even the kids were silent, content with the direction our lives were taking.

I will never forget the phone call that awakened me before sunrise the next morning, Monday, January 30, 1971.

"Hello, Annick? This is Walter."

"Walter, who?" I asked, trying to shake some waking dream.

"This is Walter, and I'm afraid I've got bad news." It was too early for bad news.

His next words came in loud and clear. "The house burned down. We come to feed the cows this morning, and there was nothing left but the ashes."

As all of us slept, the storm had whirled and gusted with lightning, thunder, and driving rain, and in the ranch house the fire the Vannoys left smoldering in the barrel stove got away out of control.

"Or maybe it was the wiring," said Walter.

No one saw the house burn down except the cows in their stalls, who must have shrunk back from the blazing light.

Damage control was my domain. I drove to the ruins with the insurance adjuster. Walter was right. Not a log remained. The out-of-focus Polaroids the adjuster took as evidence of loss show a cement-lined hole that had been the root cellar; the brick chimney red against snow and smoking ash; and me in a yellow slicker, looking down at the mess. I carried one of those photos in my wallet for years, until I lost the wallet. It was my *memento mori*—a reminder of fate. It seemed nothing would ever work right for us again.

ロ   ロ   ロ

Barn swallows cry in alarm and circle as their meticulously crafted mud-dauber nests fall from a high eave to shatter on the ground. I wonder if they grieve. How quickly they quit their crying and rebuild. I am tempted to see purpose in their acts, a will like my own. Or are they simply puppets to a genetically coded program? Either way, I doubt if you could stop their toil.

Humans are not much different. After the old house burned down, we used our twelve thousand dollars of insurance money to put up a new one in the midst of our meadow. We did not build it from scratch; our house is recycled. Dave and I found the actual house of our dreams while trout fishing where the Big Blackfoot joins the North Fork south of Ovando.

Massive even at a distance, it was an abandoned log house that sat on a field of sagebrush and wild iris like a mirage of the good life. The walls were made of hewn logs a foot and a half wide and twenty-six feet long. They had been squared with a broad ax and adze, fitted together with dovetail joints. With two full stories, a steeply pitched gabled roof, and a lean-to kitchen, the structure was the wilderness translation of a Midwestern farmhouse. Families had lived there since the turn of the century, and we found newspapers from the forties stuffed into cracks as insulation. The absentee owner, a dentist in Moses Lake, wanted to burn the house down for an extra acre of pasture land. We were the only ones who saw its promise.

We bought the house for two hundred dollars and the outbuildings for one hundred. Dave and I camped nearby all of June, living in a sky-blue six-person wall tent with our four boys, a Siamese cat, a German Shepherd, and a black Lab puppy named Shy Moon. Jon came to help us. By the campfire one starlit evening, he taught the older boys to chug Jim Beam. The next morning they were pale and wobbly but hard at work, initiated into the rites of mountain manhood.

Together, we tore the old house down. With mallets and crowbars, Jon, Eric, and Steve smashed the plastered walls and dismembered the roof beams. Dave and I pulled nails, carefully saving the weathered, hand-milled siding to use again as interior panels. Then we stamped a number into each log, matching the numbers to diagrams Dave drew. We would rebuild the house like a giant's Lincoln Log puzzle on our own property thirty miles downriver.

That June was a blessed season, all of us living out-of-doors, the twins barefoot and sunburnt. We fished in the Blackfoot for breakfast trout, and bathed in it after work. At sunset we got out baseball mitts, bats and a ball and played pickup softball on the sagebrush flat.

Friends came for the Fourth of July weekend to help stack the heavy, hand-hewn logs onto the Vannoy's logging truck. We hauled the whole house and a barn and a blacksmith's shed back to Bear Creek in three loads. After the fireworks, we celebrated with a picnic of hot dogs, potato salad, watermelon, and beer. Like the Swedes who homesteaded our piece of ground and the unknown pioneers on the Blackfoot who had created an American Gothic farmhouse out of virgin timbers, we were going to build our own home on our own land.

"Watch out," I have warned friends who speak lightly about building a house. "If you build it, be sure you want it. The place will own you." We settled the huge timbers carefully into place, fitting each into perfect dovetail joints.

ᴄ   ᴄ   ᴄ

May 8, 1974, was a warm wildflower day. The first thing we did that morning was watch a hawk. The hawk landed on the very top of a snag at the edge of our meadow. Below, in wild roses, crows had been tearing at the remains of a gopher. The hawk was big and had a white breast. An immature red-tail, we thought, or an adult ferruginous. He took his time. His waiting frightened the crows away.

The morning opened blue and green. We could not work indoors. We went for a walk. David felt strong. I saw no sign of his recurrent despair. His face was clear and tan, his eyes tender—blue as the bluebirds flitting around the eaves of our house. Have you ever noticed how the blue of the male seems to come from inside? How it takes your eye and dominates?

We walked past the run-off cattail pond near the cattle guard that separates our meadow from the pine forest.

Frogs leaped, rippling the ditch water. The wind came up.
Usually Dave did not like wind. But this day it was good.
We had lived in Los Angeles from October until the end
of March in an against-the-odds gamble to break into
Hollywood as screenwriters. But luck had not come
knocking. Homesick and broke, we returned to Montana
with the spring birds. Dave welcomed this fresh breeze
that cleared out the smog and defeat still trapped in his
lungs and heart. We headed down the logging road
toward Bear Creek.

"Creek's down," said Dave, but it was still at flood.
Run-off snow waters gushed through the culvert under the
road into a gravel-bedded pool alive with a school of fin-
gerling trout. Trout reminded us of our friend, the poet
Richard Hugo, a bait fisherman with a roaring laugh and
a heart as massive as his great round head.

"We'll have to tell Dick he's welcome to fish here any-
time," said Dave.

Our road continued upward at a steady grade. We
never slackened our pace. I stopped at a viewpoint to catch
my breath and looked down at the ranch through the tops
of ponderosas and the feathery new-green needles of western larch.

"It's not as spectacular as the Missions," said Dave,
referring to the dreamscape of high white peaks in the
Flathead Valley, "but we've got our paradise." It was good
to be home. Once we had made love at this spot, me standing with my back to the view. We had, in fact, coupled
many times in the woods. After fights, on riding jaunts,
picking wildflowers in Bear Cove, hunting for morels
under dead leaves.

Only a pause. We walked uphill, faster than before.

"Don't you feel anything?" I asked, my breath getting short again. I was thinking about Dave's heart and the expected pain of angina.

"No, I think I'm getting better."

I thought so, too. We strode away, talking about the future. We were ready for yet another new start. Dave had celebrated his forty-first birthday four days before. "One step down," six-year-old Andrew had cracked as his dad blew out the candles.

Dave had applied for a job the Friday before, to start an educational television station in Montana. It would be a job that could use the skills he had learned as a lawyer, a professor, a filmmaker. He liked to be the energy behind beginnings. Dave was never good at finishing. That was my forte. "You need to be more of a self-starter," he would say. "You take your life too much from me."

Dave was right. It was my habit to follow in his tracks, picking up any work I could get—teaching, editing, community planning, making documentary films. I would look for a job, too. "Don't short-change yourself," said Dave, getting angry at the mere chance of me doing what I had usually done. "If you can't get twelve thousand dollars, don't take anything. Wait for the right opportunity."

Two years, we agreed. Two years would get the new life going and then we'd return to the movie-making dream with money in the bank, the ranch house finished, and a "track record" in the media business. We needed to disentwine our lives. He to work on his own, perhaps commute on weekends from Helena. It would be back to the old Dave, the fair-haired country boy who wanted to be a man in the world. Nice clothes. Fast new car. No more middle-aged dropout. No invalid. No underground man writing desperately in a freezing cabin or in a Hollywood hole so disreputable we would not ask our friends to dinner. I would hire a proper babysitter. Build a fieldstone fireplace for the house and decks on three sides. We would go on expeditions. Host parties. Free ourselves from constant childcare and hand labor. We spun daydreams as we walked. Next summer we would go back to England, where the twins had been born, back to Spain, where Dave had discovered his illness. We'd do it with dollars in our pockets, Hemingway style, and have a grand reunion in Paris with the Seattle crowd we called the Magnificent Seven.

This was the moment to begin more independent lives, our bond intact. We would end the contention that devoured our energies and dissipated our affections. Dave would spend time alone with the older boys. In July, he would take them on a pilgrimage to their Midwestern roots. Let Eric and Steve meet their father's blood kin— pioneer stock from the Minnesota Bible belt—farmers, greenhouse owners, small-town Americans.

They would visit his mother, Virtue, in Hastings. She was the town crazy, the Smith family's black sheep who lived in a shack without gas or water through the subzero Minnesota winter. Virtue was paralyzed with schizophrenia and the shame of bearing four children from four fathers (three of the children, including Dave, illegitimate). She had pains in her chest and spent her days on a couch reinventing the past. Her main obsession was to unite Dave with the Swedish farmer who had fathered him, then abandoned mother and child so he could marry a proper woman and raise a proper family. In boyhood, Dave had crossed paths with his father many times in Hastings.

They never spoke. Virtue's schemes enraged her son, yet filled him with pity. This would be Dave's last free summer with Eric, who was graduating high school and ready to fly off to South America. Long-haired Steve, at sixteen, was claiming his own independence. We had reached the high point of the logging road, which dipped away toward the mouth of Bear Creek. We could see the ice-blue creek waters flowing into the turgid Big Blackfoot a mile below us and north.

◻   ◻   ◻

Going back was easy. Downhill most of the way. On a logged-off hillside, clumps of yellow balsamroot brought sun-color into the dark woods. A raincloud passed over and cooled our faces with a windy drizzle. "I like the rain," I said.

"It's all right," said Dave, "as long as we don't get soaked."

We stopped to pick sunflowers and a bunch of lupine, profuse and blue on the slopes. Wild violets sprouted along the roadside in greater numbers than I had ever seen, and we added them to our bouquet, recalling lines from Wordsworth: "A violet 'neath a mossy stone . . . " But the thousands of delicate golden glacier lilies, misnamed dog-tooth violet, were fading. They had always been our favorite.

The previous evening we had taken Dick Hugo and his soon-to-be wife, Ripley Schemm, for an after-dinner stroll up our meadow and into the woods. Dick had lagged behind, huffing, limping. A life of alcohol and cigarettes,

ulcers, too much weight, and weakness from a recent operation were taking their toll. "You'll have to get in shape,
Dick," Dave had called down from his path as leader, feeling solicitous. When Hugo reached the woods we showed
him the ground-covering glacier lilies with the pointed
common name.

"I will put dog-tooth violet in a poem," said Dick.
We had led him to poems before, led him to one of his
greatest, "Degrees of Gray in Philipsburg," a poem that
emerged from a day of filming our first movie, a movie
about Hugo.

Now, as we crossed over the cattle guard and onto our
property, Dave and I stopped to admire the house we'd
built. It seemed to grow out of the velvet green meadow.
The hewn logs, white-striped chinking, and cedar roof
absorbed the late morning sun. The huge structure had
taken two years of dedicated labor, and it was not finished.
"I can't go inside," said Dave. "Let's work on the ditches."

That day the study remained empty. No writing, no
typing. Dave taught me how to change the gravity-flow
irrigation channels with a shovel or two of sod. Sod is mag-
ical. It takes root wherever you put it down, joining itself to
the earth. Yet it is light and easy to dig. Not like the hard
clay beneath.

We fixed the gate leading to our outbuildings so the
horses could not get into the hayfield. A perfectionist, Dave
insisted the job be done right. He pounded metal stakes
with a six-pound sledge. "Let me have a turn," I insisted.

"No, I feel fine." When Dave lifted the heavy metal
frame into place, I could see him wince from the angina
pains in his left arm. My stomach cried lunch, but Dave
wanted to scout the southeast portion of the meadow and

repair a ditch trampled by last year's cattle. I fetched him in at two o'clock. "I thought it was only about noon," Dave laughed, not wanting to stop.

When Dave dug an old *Life* article about Ernest Hemingway out of his files, I knew euphoria had returned. "The Hem" had always been one of his heroes. Our friend Jim Welch called about plans for an opening-day fishing party and camp-out. It would be like our first good Montana times, with many friends we had not seen for nearly a year. Dave was feeling so well he even talked about reorganizing the old English Department softball team. It makes me weep to remember the high hopes of that afternoon. We cooked up plans for a Midsummer Eve celebration. A homecoming, a housewarming. "I'll write Eric Johnson today," said Dave, "and you write Justine."

Later in the afternoon, Dave took out the .22 rifle we had given him for his birthday and went up the meadow to shoot gophers. He and the older boys were counting, and he had to get even with Steve. I washed the windows as a welcoming gesture to spring, and for my parents who were to arrive from Chicago next day. At three-thirty, I climbed into our second-hand Ford to meet the twins at the school-bus stop on the highway. Eric and Steve were at a concert kegger to usher in spring with bluegrass and beer. I waved so-long to the yellow sweater high in the meadow. A yellow-sheathed arm waved back. It was a happy day. None better.

Dave was irrigating the lower meadow when we came back. I cooked a good stew using the beef we had raised on our grass and slaughtered in the fall. Dinner would be at six, on time and rich with wine and garlic. I started my letter to Justine.

At six o'clock exactly (I looked at the clock), he came in. Blue Levi's, jean jacket, old yellow sweater, and black irrigating boots. I had just addressed my envelope to Blue Hill, Maine. Dave nodded hello to me and the twins, who were playing on the hardwood floor with their little men. He was tired from a day's work in the sun. "Dinner's ready," I said.

Dave went to the sink in the kitchen to wash up. Turning to me (I will always see him turning), he softly said, "Oh dear" (I will hear the words always). His blue eyes widened. He doubled over for an instant, then fell hard and straight on his face. He did not put his hands out to break his fall. I ran to him. The bridge of his nose was cut. It bled. He was unconscious. Run to the phone. Call the ambulance. No time for directions. Run back to him. Two gasps and a final heaving. Too late. He is gone. Alex cries. Andrew sits quiet on the stairs. Scream "Oh David. Poor David. Oh, oh, David."

I try to bring him back. A half-hour good-bye kiss— mouth-to-mouth resuscitation. I pound his chest sixty times a minute. "Heart massage," the ambulance people told me. No use.

Later the doctor said "arrhythmia," said "fibrillation." Said David must have had a minor heart attack that day or the day before. No way to save him except in a hospital twenty-five miles away. Hold two metal paddles over the heart. Jolts of electricity spark the muscle. Get it beating. We knew the procedure. Years before, we had made a Super-8 film about defibrillation.

    ◧   ◧   ◧

Snow fell the next morning, and I awoke from my first
night of grief to find six elk grazing on new meadow grass,
pawing the wet snow under my living-room window. We
held a wake at the ranch. Neighbors I knew only slightly
brought macaroni casseroles, banana bread, a sliced ham.
The cardiologist's wife wore white gloves. Her husband
had convinced me to approve an autopsy, "not for your
sake," he said, "for the boys." Now he pulled me aside. "It's
a wonder Dave kept going at all." It seems his coronary
arteries were shrunken to half normal size, like a withered
arm, from a birth defect. It must have been stubbornness
that kept him moving. I was glad Dave had spent his last
days fishing, walking our hills, and irrigating our meadows, absorbed in doing what he loved most.

Dick Hugo wrote Dave's eulogy and read it through
tears over a grave planted near flowering lilacs: "No poet
uttered a more profound truth than Pound when he said
'What thou lovest well remains.' In our minds we know
David is dead, but in some far more important region of
self we can think of him only as living."

Now Dick is gone too, his headstone in the old
Missoula cemetery not far from where we buried David.
The spirits of Dave and Dick look out at a working-class
neighborhood like the ones they grew up in, with a full
view of the Northside softball diamond. The sport they
played together and loved keeps going spring after spring
with friends called Snake and Buddha and The Doctor,
with our own sons in the outfield—the new generations.

This is what remains. My boys are grown and mostly
gone. I live on my homestead, alone some nights and some
nights with my longtime companion, Bill Kittredge, a man
I love and cherish. I have a shepherd dog and her mongrel

pup, a black-and-white cat the twins brought home from
Cincinnati, and two mares that Dave and I used to race
across our meadows. Neighbors help me cut and stack hay
each summer, and I toss bales from the loft of the log barn
to feed the horses each winter. Almaree is the lame old
chestnut quarterhorse with the gray muzzle; Eustacia, her
red foal, was born in a spring blizzard the month we
moved onto our land. The horses are old and fat now, and
wild, and I don't ride them anymore, but those horses have
come to own the land as much as I do.

From the wide kitchen windows we built ourselves, I
love to watch my horses top the ridge and graze their way
down toward the house. Most of the windows are cracked.
The fir frames were too green when we fitted them with
double panes of glass, and one hot August Sunday four
windows gave way, perhaps from pressure as the logs settled on their new foundation. The sounds of glass cracking
were like shots from a rifle.

◧   ◧   ◧

A couple of years after Dave died, I dreamed of my Victorian
house again. It was a warm full-moon night in July, too hot
for blankets. The kids were gone to visit my parents in
their summer house on Lake Michigan, and I was alone,
feeling abandoned in the high, empty bedroom with its
skylight above the double bed and tall, uncurtained windows looking out to the meadows. The Bear Creek Valley
and the pine-forested hills glowed soft, muted blue. I tossed
a long time in my moonlit bed before falling into sleep.

The house I entered was familiar, but somehow sinis-
ter. Its rooms were a rambling maze, and I was lost in their

turnings. The lower story was walled with stone, the windows leaded, walls paneled in mahogany, and window seats upholstered in velvet.

I was not content to sit in my usual place and look out at gardens of poppies and roses. I was searching for David. I climbed staircase after staircase and finally arrived at my bedroom in the tower. The many-sided room was full of sunlight, and I breathed easier. I heard laughter and wandered to a window. Outside, tall as the house, was an apple tree in full bloom. I opened the window, leaned out to pick white blossoms. But I could not reach the bough.

A man sat in the highest branches. It was David, blue-eyed, blond as he had been when I first knew him, but he was not a boy anymore. I called to him. He did not answer. He smiled, though, and I knew he was happy. He was smiling at me.

I awoke feeling comforted. I heard the odd, creaking talk of swallows building their mud-dauber nests under the peaked eaves of our roof. Early morning sun slid into open windows. I was at home, and not alone. Out by the stone pile a long-eared coyote cried the day alive. We can never be abandoned. The love you have had will never abandon you.

Generations

It shocks me to recognize that I am not the individualist I thought I was. By choosing to live my adult life in Montana I have aped my parents in spite of myself. Like them I emigrated to a land of greater freedom. Like them I rooted my life in art and rooted my art to a chosen place. Like them I valued family to the detriment of career. Looking toward their deaths and my old age, I am compelled to come to terms with the bitter and the sweet of our shared past.

My maiden name is Deutsch. My parents are Jewish children of the Austro-Hungarian Empire. My father's father, Gyla Deutsch, fought in World War I on the German side. His forefathers from the tribes of Israel, when they finally settled in the land of the Magyars, had been branded with the name of the conquering Hun as surely as his cousins would be branded with numbers in Auschwitz. The name meant *You belong to Germany!*

Deutsch. Our old name shudders from the weight of conquest and genocide. But the new one is more complex. In 1937, soon after I was born, my parents came from Paris to join my father's mother and father and his older brother in Chicago. They held a family council. In this free country you could change your name, so they excised the letter *s*, leaving history behind. Which is what my father wanted.

All through our grade-school years, my younger sisters and I tried to pry stories of Budapest out of him.

"I have nothing interesting to tell you." Father was stony. He did not want to talk about the past. He wanted all of us to be assimilated. Luckily my uncle Gene and my father Stephen did not change their last name to Davis or Brown, which was the way some immigrant Jews looked for safety in the New World. They did not turn Episcopalian. The Deutch brothers fathered six girls, and their colonial name ends with my sisters and cousins and me. They believed a new American story would begin with us.

⊏   ⊏   ⊏

In the rambling apartment where I grew up, three stories above Lakeside Street on Chicago's North Side, I would lie on my parents' bed and study photograph albums. The bed was strange and illicit, charged with sexual energies, the perfumes of my parents' bodies. The pictures in the albums were even stranger. There was a skeletal great-grandmother in a babushka, her old man holding his black hat. I felt no connection to those country people—peasants really—weathered and lined, tinted sepia. They were gnomes out of Grimm's Fairy Tales.

I heard whispers that gypsy genes had darkened my Grandma Deutch's bloodline. That was swell by me. My first Halloween costume was whirling skirts, golden earrings, a tambourine. I was five. I remember pelting my sister with flowers. When I asked Grandma, "Are we part gypsy?" her answer was emphatically no. If poor country Jews were on the low end of the Hungarian social ladder, gypsies were the bottom rung. Being gypsy, however, like being French, was a story I needed to believe in. I was creating the romance of myself, and to this day I ascribe my nomadic ways, longing for wildness, and disdain of material belongings to blood that is partways gypsy.

In another photo, my grandfather, Gyla, stands erect in his World War I uniform amid a company of soldiers. He is stern and handsome with a full mustache. This was not the gruff old man who pulled my sleigh through drifts in Lincoln Park. The Grandpa Deutch I knew had a face pocked with scars from an incurable skin disease he contracted during the war, and his nose was bulbous, veined, and red from too much schnapps. To find the man behind the old photograph and decipher my father's story, I would have to time-travel back to the city of Pest, across the Danube from the medieval castles and hills of Buda.

In 1908, when my father was born, Pest was a spanking modern city spread out on sandy river-bottom plains. Grandpa Deutch was a handyman who sometimes cobbled shoes. Johanna, my grandmother, was called *Honi-nani* (Aunt Jo), or just plain Honi. Her wedding portrait shows a small, round-eyed, buxom woman laced into white satin. She was my favorite. When I knew her, she was all round, five by five, slowed by rheumatism but sharp-witted and quick to laugh. I associate Grandma Deutch with honey and bees. She was enveloped in the scent of violets.

Pista (pronounced Pishta—a diminutive for Stephen or Istvan), my father, was the youngest of three sons. He grew up in a cramped apartment above a men's social club on Andrassy Avenue, the main street of Pest. In my fantasies, I had placed my father's family in a ghetto like Warsaw's, thick with odors of cabbage and horse manure. It served my sense of myself to see my kin as victims of pogroms, living in a warren with stone walls to keep the Jews in their place.

Now, as we talk in my parents' Chicago apartment, twenty-six stories above Lake Shore Drive, my father sits in a therapeutic chair. At eighty-six, he has just undergone surgery that replaced his arthritic left shoulder joint with a titanium ball and socket. A mechanical device raises his left arm to shoulder height, then slowly brings it down. My ignorance makes him smile.

"No," he says. "It was like living on Fifth Avenue."

"The Champs-Elysee," my mother interjects.

Andrassy Street was 140 feet wide and paved with hardwood blocks. There were covered walkways with marble arches. Artists and intellectuals lounged in glass-walled open-air cafes called "Japan" and "New York." Under the clink of silver, you might hear the rattle and hum of the Franz Josef Underground Line, the world's first electric subway. Built in 1869, the cars ran through a square tunnel.

Father's family lived rent free in the apartment on Andrassy Avenue because my grandfather was caretaker of the social club below, whose members were Jewish merchants. Grandma served coffee. Her three sons helped with the work. Childhood photos of my father show a cocky, skinny kid with a shaved head, large nose, and ears not yet grown into.

"Your grandfather would beat your father if he did not go to temple," says Mother. Father took the beatings. He preferred Sabbath soccer to religion, and still does. In Chicago, while my grandparents were alive, my family humored them with Passover suppers: fingers dipped in wine, the Hebrew prayers chanted, matzo ball soup. As the eldest child, I was allowed to open the front door to allow the Prophet to enter. I loved the ritual, the mystery of it.

But my sisters and I never went inside a temple or church except to view the art or hear the music. "Look at the light," my father instructed. It seems we children were always to look at the light.

At twelve, my father quit school and went to work as an apprentice woodcarver. "That was when I decided to sleep on the billiard table," he says.

I ask him why. "It was macho. I thought I was a tough guy." Father grins with rare self-irony. "The pool table was hard. I slept on it for two years."

The pride of pain is something my father understands. When he retired at age seventy-five from his work as a commercial photographer, he went back to the art of his youth. He carved figures out of hardwood until the pain in his shoulders grew so great he could not lift his hammer to strike the chisel. Father clenches his teeth and holds to his machismo, except when he weeps. Music makes him weep. Bach. And Mascagni's *Cavalleria Rusticana*. And a soaring, wailing Missa Flamenco he plays over and over on the tape deck. Everything about my father is excess: the love I duck away from as he holds my face in two hands; his perpetual sadness; a stubborn self-reliance that makes it impossible for him to receive any gift with grace; and what I call hunger—his unsated desire for beauty and more beauty. This he passed on to me—a hunger that has informed my life, driving me west, always west toward what I see as light.

Even as a teenager, my father had an affinity for wood. He apprenticed himself to a woodcarver and performed so well that a wealthy uncle paid his way to the Royal Academy of Fine Arts. There he learned the classic styles, imitating Roman busts, Greek gods, and nymphs. But the art that took my father's imagination was not classic but modern.

In choosing an artist's craft, my father was following in the wake of his brothers. Alfred, six years older, was a lean and serious young man who worked his way through a commercial college and became an illustrator and designer of Art Deco objects. Gene, the handsome, fun-loving middle son, became a renowned ceramics artist. When Gene died of cancer at fifty-five, several pieces of his work had been purchased by the Art Institute of Chicago for its permanent collection. I wonder how those sons of a janitor came to such ambition? No doubt they were touched by the leftist revolutions of 1918 and 1919, when the dual monarchy toppled and for 132 days Bela Kun, a Jewish Communist, ruled the capitol. During the twenties the city came alive again with commerce, poetry, and music. I am astonished at the numbers of Hungarian artists—such a small country, so arrogant. Perhaps art was in the air—the leafy, violet-scented air of *fin de siècle* Budapest.

But in the Age of the Moderne the action was in Paris. In 1926, at eighteen, my father left home, his first emigration. I wonder how he must have felt, a poor Hungarian boy in the City of Lights. I think he loved it, knew Paris was home, exalted in the energies of youth and art. On the Left Bank a few years later he met a fellow émigré, Helene Beck, my mother.

◲ ◲ ◲

Mother buys me fifty-dollar face cream. She wants me to be her slim, black-haired girl. But I am nearly sixty and sturdy

as the flesh around my bones. I flaunt my white mane like a
flag, until Mother's critical eye gives me the once-over. We
look at each other bewildered. Neither of us is comfortable
with the transformations of age.

My mother is heading toward ninety years. She is
smaller than I remembered, more fragile. I must bend low
to kiss her soft face. We stand in the apartment of my parents' old age. April light from the bay windows is white
with humidity. Lake Michigan is Easter-egg blue. I look
down on Wrigley Field and the soot-covered roofs of
Chicago.

I have flown to the city of my girlhood from Montana,
where for more than half my life I have denned in my log
house on a mountain meadow, dreamy as a silver-tip bear.
I am happy in Montana because it holds me in a continual
present, time flowing like spring weather, wildflowers
today, sleet tomorrow. Chicago, on the other hand, is a trip
back to mortality.

The three-room apartment is hung like a museum
with artifacts from my family's history. The friends who
painted the cubist dancer, the watercolor of a 1940s
Chicago street, are dead. Free-form ceramic ashtrays,
lamps and swan-like bowls made by Uncle Gene, dead
forty years, sit on every flat surface. My father's wood
sculptures of nudes and accordian players, Adam and Eve,
are reminiscent of Henry Moore. Yet my eyes fasten upon a
woman's face that emerges from a rough-hewn slab depict-
ing the Holocaust. Her mouth is contorted into a scream.

How do you speak truly about your mother without
deceit, with open loving eyes? Why speak at all? I tell my
mother's story because I am her daughter. I live the life my
mother would have lived if she could have imagined it. I

travel on writing assignments to Bristol Bay, the Salton Sea, Andalusia. I have made films and hobnobbed with Robert Redford. Mother loves the natural world I live in day to day, but she could not tolerate Montana winters—the edge of insecurity that keeps me on my toes.

When my parents emigrated to America, they carried the baggage of the Old World. Family was primary, patriarchal, powerful. We lived in a house full of women—Mother, my Grandma Beck, three sisters, and my father. He was the star around whom we revolved. I thought I was his clone because he took me into the world like an eldest son. I followed his lead in books, politics, music, and baseball, until I grew self-aware enough to understand that the person I most resemble at my emotional core is Mother. When I tell tales about my mother I'm telling tales on me. It is a way to free myself in some degree from the family myths that gave me cause for a lifelong struggle. I want my children to embrace new myths in which Mother and Father are not godlike and women are equal players who do not resort to feminine deceptions that diminish and degrade.

Mother comes from Transylvania. When she lived there in the early 1900s it was an agricultural land full of vineyards, feudal estates, and peasant farms in the foothills of the Carpathian Mountains. Before the era of politically correct language, Mother identified herself as a "white Jew" because of the German blood on her father's side. She has always been proud of her even features, soft light hair, and unlined skin, which could allow her to pass for Aryan any place on earth. If you ask her secret, Mother will laugh and say, "Pond's Cold Cream."

My mother's real name is Ilona Beck, which should be translated Elaine. Her first name, and at least one year of her age (a fact she vigorously denies), were left behind when, at eighteen, she got a visa to emigrate to France. To the Hungarian-hating Rumanians who had taken over her country, Elaine sounded like Helene, so what the hell, you're changing countries, you may as well have a new name.

Mother is well under five feet tall and dainty. Humped from osteoporosis, the child she was has emerged like a small butterfly with milk white hair. Other women may become what she disdainfully refers to as "old ladies," but she, never. A son-in-law used to call her Bride of Frankenstein. When we want to get Mother's goat, we call her Zsa Zsa.

While Father naps, Mother and I sit in the living room and talk in soft voices. The couch where we lounge and the padded Eames chairs have been upholstered by her sure hands. In her old age and my middle age, we have come closer. This intimate moment is a time for storytelling, and if my mother likes anything better than gourmet cooking, it is telling stories of her childhood.

When they were my age, my parents went back to Hungary. The streets of my father's home in Budapest were somber under Soviet rule. Liberation had been hibernating, but the stones of the city remained familiar. You could walk amid memories. Not so in Mother's hometown of Nagyvarad, meaning "Big Fortress," after the ruined towers that once held back the Turks. Mother's birthplace had become victim to Rumania's Soviet-inspired idea of progress — the destruction of all things Hungarian, Catholic, old.

"I tried to find the house we lived in," she says. "I could not even find the street. They have built cement apartments there. It is ugly." There are tears in Mother's eyes. Ugliness is sin number one. "The beautiful river where we swam—I wanted to show your father."

A river runs through Nagyvarad, a town I imagine as a Hungarian version of Missoula, the center of my life these thirty years, split by the trout-rich Clark Fork River. Odd, I think, that instinct has led me to a home so like my mother's. Mother used to swim in the city pool that was built into her town's river. The waters were so clear you could dive in and see boulders on the sandy bottom, and so swift only the strongest could swim upstream. In winter my mother and her friends would skate on the river.

"It was gone." Mother's voice drops as she remembers. Age diminishes all things. It has softened her voice to a whisper.

"Brown. There was oil, like rainbows, on the top. The trees are gone. The fish. It is polluted."

I barely hear her last word. "Destroyed . . ."

The Beck family lived a bourgeois life in a spacious house near a park. My grandfather, Henrik, managed an insurance brokerage, but because he was Jewish he could not own it or advance in the company. Still, the Becks were middle-class and always had a maid. Each room in the Victorian household held a hand-painted tile stove.

I imagine my grandmother's whitewashed kitchen, redolent with odors of her fine Hungarian cooking like the kitchens she ruled in my childhood: chicken paprika; veal goulash; stuffed peppers; apple strudel; and a fragrant yeast bread, something like American Indian fry bread, which Grandma Beck called *langosz*. "Now, eat." A litany passed from generation to generation.

I see Mother's childhood in embroidery, delicate as the

lace tablecloths Grandma Beck stitched in our Chicago
living room those long evenings before television, when
we gathered around the hi-fi to listen to Bach and do
our homework. I see hand-sewn ruffled dresses and long
curls, young Ilush in her party gown. Pretty. Pristine.
My sister Kathy and I used to speculate about the sexual lives of our mother and father, as little girls do, trying
to figure out what a woman should be. We acted out soap
operas with our paper dolls, whispered and giggled over
hot scenarios of married life. We wanted to be sexy, like
our father. He slept naked. I remember staring at his genitals those mornings I caught him walking down the hall
from bedroom to bathroom. When he kissed me I pulled
away, the touch too dangerous. All my friends had crushes
on Stephen Deutch, the photographer who took pictures of
models and movie stars. When we were teens my sisters
and I came to believe he had affairs with some of those
women. And when we were grown, he confirmed our sus-
picions by running off with a blonde named Zee, who had
a southern accent.

I never could pin down my mother's sexual nature.
There was a kittenish side to her, teasing rather than sexy.
At the cocktail parties we had at our house I could see that
men were attracted to her. Sometimes our parties ended in
drunken dancing, my father wild as anyone, my sisters and
me getting high on the guests' forgotten Scotch-and-soda
highballs. But I cannot remember Mother doing anything
rash or indiscreet.

Mother's daintiness made her seem squeamish and
Victorian to a rebel daughter in worn jeans, men's white
shirts, and bare feet. I preferred not to imagine my mother
abandoned in the sweaty, smelly contacts of passion. But

snapshots from her Paris high-jinx days show a young woman with a come-on look — a woman who flaunted her round breasts and slender legs. I ask myself, what do I really comprehend about the interior life of my mother? What I know is Mother was repulsed in childhood by male genitals. Her fear goes back to a day when she was five.

"I was playing with my cat," she tells me. "The cat ran into a small shed behind our house where the man lived who tended our yard — the gardener, you know — that kind of man. He was always nice to me. But he was old and dirty. And he smelled."

Mother wrinkles her freckled nose. If ugliness is sin number one in her lexicon, bad smells are sin number two.

"I did not think. I followed the cat. The man was sitting in a chair right in back of the open door. His pants was open. He was pulling his penis . . . up and down."

Mother stops a moment to catch her breath. She makes a terrible face. "It was big. And sticking up out of his pants like a snake. It was moving. He called to me. 'Come here,' he said. 'Come touch it. It won't bite you.'"

Eighty years later, she shudders. "I ran away. I never forget that."

Sexual organs may have been repulsive to the girl, Ilona, but death was a greater horror. Mother is haunted by mortality. Her father died of sudden kidney failure when she was thirteen. She has witnessed the deaths of two sons-in-law, many friends, the slow arthritic crippling of my father. When her ninety-three-year-old mother lay dying in the hospital, Mother stayed faithfully at her side until the nurse and doctors and my father convinced her to go home and get some rest. Grandma Beck died in her sleep that night. "I let my mother die all alone," she says, swept by guilt. The question in Mother's eyes makes me want to look away. You won't do that to me, will you? she is asking. You won't let me die with no one to hold my hand?

ᴇ   ᴇ   ᴇ

The family beans I have been spilling are about sex and death. Yet when I examine the patchwork of my mother's life, the most knotted threads are the puzzle of self-realization. All her life, Mother has struggled against the domination of others. She resorts to female strategies of the powerless passed on through female generations: charm, humor, manipulation, willfulness, hysteria. She first perfected these weapons in an underground war against *her* mother.

Grandma Beck was a manager by nature. In her Hungarian household, the only keys to the locked pantry hung on her belt. Grandma's name was Serena, but she was a far way from serene. A widow at forty, she was still handsome at ninety-three. Her mind was quick, her hands skilled. She bundled her long, white hair in a bun and died with her natural teeth.

The one person I cannot imagine Grandma trying to boss was my stolid and studious Uncle Jean. After his father died, Jean went to France to study at the Sorbonne. He earned a doctorate in biology. He married a French girl of peasant stock and had a daughter named Helene, after my mother. Jean Beck would become a Frenchman and a professor of science.

As soon as Mother finished high school, Grandma Beck packed their belongings and set off with her daughter for Paris, so they could be with Jean. They went poor because the Rumanian government had cheated Grandma out of most of her husband's insurance, and money from the sale of their house was not allowed to leave the country. With her small savings and a hat full of bitterness, my grandmother left her homeland and never came back.

Mother went to the Sorbonne for two years. She had boyfriends, skied in Switzerland, went on white-water canoe parties. Then she discovered photography. There was a chance meeting with a Hungarian photographer friend of her brother's. The young man needed money to start a business. My grandmother invested five thousand francs. When no profit came of it, Mother was sent to La Place d'Etoile to investigate.

The business failed, but during her inspections, Mother learned about cameras and lighting, developing and retouching. Retouching would be her specialty. Mother was a retoucher for *Vogue* during its Paris heyday. At twenty, she worked under the fashion photographers and became an assistant, then a full-fledged shooter. She posed models in Chanel suits, retouched negatives to create the illusion of perfection. But no matter how *au courant* and flapperish she became, young Helene remained firmly tied to the apron strings of her widowed mother.

Serena Beck could have married again. Many widows remarried. For her, such a choice was unthinkable. I remember the day she lost her gold wedding ring down the bathroom drain in our Chicago apartment. I was eleven. We poked a bent wire hanger down the sinkhole. The ring was gone into Chicago sewers. Grandma Beck held my hand. Her skin was soft as butter.

"I wish you could have known your grandfather

Henrik," she said. "He was so nice to me." This was a reprimand. My father, my sisters, and me — we were not so nice. I tried to pull my hand away. Tears ran down her wrinkled cheeks. Fifty years had passed, and still she wept when she spoke her dead husband's name.

"Annickam, I miss him always so much." Grandma's English was broken with French and Hungarian words from her fractured life, but there was little sympathy I could give her, for I despised sentimentality and thought Grandma's nostalgia was a poor excuse for emotion. I imagined her as entrepreneur, running a dress shop, bossing the shopgirls instead of us. *Seren-nani* swore in Hungarian: *"Oy-yoy Ishtenem"* (Oh my God); *"Bidush kutya"* (You are a stinky dog). When all else failed she pushed me and my sisters into the broom closet.

Mother tells me I am ungrateful. From the moment I was born, she depended on Grandma's support. While Mother pursued her profession, Grandma took charge of her babies and household. After my parents emigrated to Chicago, Mother convinced Grandma to follow. The widow Beck, who had lived in her own apartment in Paris, exchanged personal freedom for a lifetime of being the third wheel in our small, contentious family.

Now I realize it was not so easy to declare independence when custom dictated such caretaking was the proper role for a widow. I am sorry I judged my grandmother too harshly, but I hold to my belief that it is safer to weep for the past than to create a new persona and try to take charge of your life.

c   c   c

All the time my mother was learning photography, my
father had been sculpting in Montmartre. He exhibited in
avant-garde shows but could not survive on art. When my
mother and father began their romance, he subsisted on
noodles, rice, and the pretzels he sold all over France and
North Africa as a traveling salesman. "Pretz-Sticks," he
says. "I wanted to see the world."

"Your father was malnourished. He had to wear a
kind of girdle," Mother says, "to hold up his intestines."

There is no evidence of a distended stomach in the
snapshots Mother took of my father as a young man. He is
slender and dark. His prominent nose is almost Egyptian.
In a double-breasted suit or tight-knit bathing outfit, he is
intense. Sad. The sadness was grief for his eldest brother,
Alfred, who had committed suicide in Chicago.

Alfred's loss is palpable after sixty years. Father opens
the door to the closet where he stores his treasures. I pull
Alfred's portfolio down from the top shelf. It is dusty. The
large pages are crumbling. I look at Alfred's designs for
Tiffany-style lamps, Art Deco fixtures for the Chicago
Opera House, and I understand my father's guilt at not
having been there when he was most needed, not being
able to help. I stood by while my young husband suffered
incurable artery disease and died. Sometimes you can help,
often you cannot.

No one knows the cause of Alfred's suicide. My
father's middle brother, Gene, might have known, for he
was with Alfred in Chicago. Gene would never say what
happened. My father fingers one of Alfred's drawings.
Whatever Gene knew was so terrifying to him that he
would get a migraine headache when my father pressed
him for answers. Sometimes he blacked out. Finally, my

father stopped asking. The Polish poet, Czeslaw Milosz, speaks of emigrants and suicide:

People decided to leave their villages and little towns in the same spirit as a man considers suicide. They weighed everything, then went off into the unknown, but once there, they were seized by a despair unlike anything they had ever experienced in the old country.

Mother helped lighten my father's grief. She gave him love and teasing laughter, taught him photography. His sculptor's eye made him an expert in lighting. They married, opened a commercial studio in Montparnasse, became French citizens, and were a hot item in the new age of advertising. I was born in May of 1936 in a small clinic in the artists' quarter. It was a good place to be born.

My father had joined the Communist Party because he believed all people should be free and economically equal. Soon after I was born he wanted to run off with the Lincoln Brigade to go fight Franco and the Nazis in Spain. Mother did not want him to leave. "You have a child," she said.

With Hitler warming up for Poland, Europe was dangerous, especially for Jews. The future lay in America. My father had offers for freelance work in New York with newly conceived *Life* magazine. I wonder what would have become of us if my father had become a photo-journalist, if my mother had stayed with high fashion. But Father's parents and brother Gene had settled in Chicago, so for the sake of family and security, in January of 1937,

we three boarded the *Isle de France* and sailed toward the
Statue of Liberty through heavy winter seas.

ᴄ   ᴄ   ᴄ

The prairie city of Chicago had become home to a large
Hungarian colony of artists fleeing German oppression.
They clustered around Maholy Nagy, a pillar of the
Bauhaus School. I like to think those Hungarians honed in
on Illinois because the land reminded them of grasslands
where horseback Magyars tended sheep. Chicago was raw
but more openhearted than the East Coast—a peasant city
I associate with heartland poets: Walt Whitman, Carl
Sandburg. And with the left-wing writers who would
become my father's friends: Studs Terkel, Gwendolyn
Brooks, Harry Petrakis, and the most dearly loved of all,
Nelson Algren.

Mother was not enchanted. She pined for her brother,
for the lightness of Paris. "Chicago was like Siberia," she
says. "The wind and the cold. The streets were so dirty."

My parents opened the Deutch Studio at 75 East
Wacker Drive in 1938. Their reputations followed from
Europe, and before long the new business prospered. The
studio was a glamourous place for my little sisters and me,
with furnishings by Herman Miller, a dressing room that
smelled of pancake makeup and the perfumes of long-
limbed models. Kathy and I played dress-up in front of the
round mirror. We painted our mouths forbidden red.

I was allowed into the darkroom to develop prints.
Under the red safety light, an alarm clock, loud as a
metronome, ticked the seconds. In an enamel pan full of
chemicals, a train took shape, an arm waved from an

open window. My father's blunt fingers were cracked from
the chemicals. His nails were turtle yellow. He bit his cuti-
cles raw.

Celebrities came to be photographed. Sonja Henie.
Barbara Rush. Joe Louis, and young Lena Horne. Duke
Ellington signed an autograph for Kathy and me, and he
kissed us full on our mouths. I had my picture taken at the
circus with the Lone Ranger. Jackie Robinson signed a
baseball for me at Wrigley Field the year he joined the
Dodgers. The photo my father snapped of Jackie and
me appeared in *Ebony*. I wore a beret with a green ribbon.
My French braids fell almost to my waist. The magic of
photography was so potent it eventually led all three of us
sisters into filmmaking.

Stone lions guarded the entrance to our three-bedroom
apartment on Lakeside Street. As part of the war effort, we
planted a Victory Garden. Only the radishes came up.
Father tried to enlist, but Uncle Sam needed photographers
at home, so he became our block's air-raid warden. By then
my father was deep into Progressive politics, having been
booted out of the Communist Party for refusing the Stalin-
ist line. Woody Guthrie and Josh White sang at a
fundraiser in our living room. The photo my father took is
black and white: a woman with padded shoulders and
page-boy hair stands by a soldier in uniform; they seem to
be standing at attention.

It's all gone—the apartment, the lions, childhood. In
our old neighborhood, new immigrants from Mexico, Asia,
American Indian reservations have replaced us European
Jews. They are the dispossessed and forgotten people my
father identified with and memorialized all through his
professional life in the portraits he made for art. Images

47

come to mind: the crouching boy at the Dixon School for Mentally Retarded Children who suppresses a silent, frozen scream; a bleached-blonde hooker in high heels at the Saucie Weenie; a stogie-mouthed Irish politician.

Mother's vision was more lighthearted. She is a master of beautiful surfaces. I remember watching her bend over a print in the studio and peer through a magnifying glass. With a fine brush she could white out wrinkles, the blemish on a woman's face. Mother believed she could perfect everything she touched—her children, her husband. But she could not keep her life from falling apart.

Memories of my childhood resound with the high pitch of fighting voices. At dinner Grandma Beck quarrelled with my father. Losing the battle, she would run to her room, weeping. Then Mother would start in, defending Grandma. The battles poisoned my parents' work. Mother might turn hysterical, but she could not be boss. So when she became pregnant with my youngest sister, Carole, she made a deal with Father. If he bought her a big house in the suburbs, she would leave the photography business to him.

◧　◧　◧

From my eighth-grade year until I went away to college I lived in Wilmette, on Chicago's North Shore. We were the first Jewish family, I'm told, to break into that lily-white burg. Mother devoted her creative talents to living the suburban dream of the 1950s. She learned to garden, play bridge, to cook and to sew; and she decorated our three-story white stucco house in high modern style, with hand-woven fabrics and Danish furniture.

Mother wanted us to fit in, too. I wore braces to push back the slightly buck teeth I had inherited from her. She sewed our clothes from Vogue patterns, but I remained foreign, different, alienated from my cashmere-clad country-club classmates. Then she started in on my large Deutch nose.

"You should get a nose job," she said. "You will look like Elizabeth Taylor."

I was obstinate. Elizabeth Taylor had blue eyes and big boobs. "Don't touch me," I said. I did not want to be improved.

Maybe it was part of the immigrant experience in the aftermath of World War II, this desire to look like your blue-eyed neighbors. Or fear of being persecuted by Senator McCarthy for being liberal, Jewish, born victims. Or the universal desire to start over fresh. Mother bought into the American media myth of the perfect family, which replaced older myths of nationality and individualism. But when Kathy and I left home the myth came crashing down. Father, distraught over his brother's death, fell in love with Gene's assistant, Zee, and Mother divorced him.

For years I ran from my mother because, like her mother, she had wrapped her life in mothballs and said it was for the sake of her children—for me. A person who perceives herself the object of someone's sacrifice cannot bear the obligation. Now I have grown children and know the temptation to live for and through your offspring. And when I see the pictures my mother created in her Paris days, my heart goes out to her, for she was an artist in her own right. There is a nude, like a doe in deep grass; and my father's backlit Egyptian profile; and a bald baby (me) in a

wicker cradle, the lawn starry with daisies. Her people
float in sunlight. When she goes, I hope to be there to hold
her hand.

เ   เ   เ

The evening before I return to Montana, I set up a screen
and projector and take out several boxes of my father's
slides. After his marriage to Zee failed he courted and
remarried my mother. Then Father embarked on a late-life
second honeymoon, his final photographic mission. He and
Mother would travel the world—India, Sicily, the Sahara,
West Africa, Poland, Japan, and of course France.

The screening is a prideful occasion for my father and
for me. While my mother turns her hearing aid down and
dozes, we mark his favorite slides to show S.O.S. We talk
about an exhibit of his art photos and sculptures that will
take place in November, a show he calls "my last hurrah,"
and his eyes fill with light, his bearing becomes charged
with the old, quick energy of ego.

As life will have it, after my father put his camera
away and turned back to sculpture, his photography
became almost famous. There have been articles about
him, documentaries for television. In 1989, when he
was eighty-one, his first book of photos, *Stephen Deutch,
Photographer,* was published to good reviews, and the
Chicago Public Library Cultural Center hosted a retro-
spective show. The Deutch collection of some thirteen
thousand transparencies, prints, and negatives dating back
to 1932 has been catalogued and stored in the Chicago
Historical Society. New generations will see the life of the
city through his eyes. Recognition sweetens the end of life,

but it does not diminish the losses. My father weeps for the loss of friends, for the loss of his manhood. He is forgetful, sometimes confused. He makes lists, writes notes to himself, nods off.

Mother remains unnoticed in the Great World, and she greets this news with a touch of bitterness. But Mother's first great-grandchild was born this summer. One is not enough. Mother is in love with babies. She wants to live amid the spawn of her blood.

When the room darkens and my father's slides click bright on the screen, I am surprised by the depth of my emotion. I love those last glowing images in full color, the dust and sand: Arabs threshing wheat; donkeys and a black-robed crone against the lime-washed walls of a Greek village; Mali dancers in feathered headdresses and white sneakers; a Provençal market stacked with luminous oranges, lemons, pears.

Lately I, too, have been traveling—to the old worlds that begat me and wild new worlds I never imagined. Restlessness lies deep in the genetic soul of our species. Like my ancestors and my progeny, I am driven by an interior green light that says "go!" We are nomads at heart, I believe, born to be hunters and gatherers. Yet when we stop to put up our tents, bear children, bury our dead, we find ourselves tied to a place on the earth we call home.

Better than Myth

There is a mythological Montana many Americans know, whether they grew up in Chicago, as I did, or in a Maine fishing village, or on the grassland ranches of Montana itself. This Montana is the dwelling place of good cowboys and bad Indians, sturdy pioneers, outlaws, and ladies of the night. It is gold, blood, and wildness—home ground for the western, which in my childhood was the dominant American myth.

When I was fourteen, I read A. B. Guthrie's *The Big Sky.* The book took me away from my suburban high school into a brilliant adventure of mountain men and Indians. I read it day and night, barely stopping to eat. Then I saw the movie *Shane,* and the West came alive with images of the Grand Tetons, white shrouded and alluring as a dream. I would look at a map of Big Sky country and the place names were magic: Virginia City, Bannock, the Little Big Horn, Yellowstone, Great Falls, Absoroke, the Bitterroots, Deer Lodge. Real names, real places, and legends.

The legend began with Lewis and Clark's 1806 voyage of exploration from Independence, Missouri, to Astoria, Oregon, and grew to huge proportions during the nineteenth century. Stories about the "Wild West" hit the

streets hot on the heels of the events they depicted. For
instance, I know of 1,700 novels written about Buffalo Bill
during his lifetime. The dime novels that popularized the
West were invented by eastern writers for the entertainment of large, urban audiences. Imagine Rambo in 1885,
but call him Wild Bill Hickok, and you will know how the
western came to be. A friend who knows once told me they
are the preferred books in jailhouse libraries.

The simplistic cowboy code that westerns refurbished
from tales of knights and dragons—good guys versus bad
guys in a ritual duel—holds great power in American
politics and foreign policy. Henry Kissinger once likened
himself to the Lone Ranger; while holding the office of
president, Ronald Reagan quoted lines from B-westerns at
the drop of a Stetson. The huge power of the National Rifle
Association lobby is connected to the almost religious belief
that no man is a real man unless he hefts a gun.

In the 1940s I would go to Sunday matinees with my
fat little Grandma Deutch and my sister Kathy. We went to
the Granada Theatre on Chicago's North Side. I was nine,
my sister seven. None of us had been west of Illinois. Still,
in the sweaty darkness of the movie house, our mouths
greasy from buttered popcorn, we three urban Hungarian
Jews would clap and cheer for the brave gunfighter, gasp
at the beauty of wild horses running free on sagebrush bad-
lands, hide our faces when grunting Apaches massacred
the blonde pioneer wife, the helpless children.

John Wayne and Gary Cooper gave face and voice
to the mythical cowboys who, we were told, "won the
West." For millions of people who watch old movies on
television, those faces, landscapes, and stories are still the
only West worth remembering. Even with a left-hand

turn for political correctness—Kevin Costner sentimental-
izing Indians as the real heroes, or the female-power *Bad
Girls*, starring Madeline Stowe, or the reluctant senior
gunfighter, Clint Eastwood, driven to revenge—westerns
continue to tantalize the American imagination.

We should know better. A vivid body of stories about
the actual mining and stockmen's frontiers exists beyond
popular novels, comic books, movies, and television. The
books I am talking about are not listed under "fiction" in
the public library; they are not "literature" in the traditional usage of that word.

◧   ◧   ◧

When I came to Missoula in 1964, I found myself free in
the afternoons for the first time in my married life. Dave,
done with graduate school, was teaching English at the
University of Montana. I had no job to run to, no babysit-
ters or preschool for the boys, no classes. I would pack Eric
and Steve off to first and third grades at the Rattlesnake
School, wash the dishes, sweep the floors, and look for
ways to entertain myself.

Often I'd take my black-and-tan German shepherd,
Sylvie, for long walks on terraced Mount Jumbo, where
coyotes and deer roamed the hillsides that are stacked with
houses now, and I would spot an occasional elk. In spring I
gathered great bouquets of yellowbells, shooting stars,
balsamroot, and lupine. In winter I went skiing with my
pediatrician's wife on Ladies' Day at Snow Bowl. When it
rained I read George Eliot and took baths in the afternoon.
And sometimes I went to the university library.

I would stand in the dark stacks in the old library's

55

basement and browse volumes of county histories collected
by local historical societies. The books were odd and personal as high school yearbooks, with family anecdotes, old
photos of rodeos and homesteaders. Each almanac had a
flavor reflecting the life of its place: wheatgrowers and
white-haired matrons from high-plains towns such as Cut-
bank; trophy elk and loggers from Superior; Crow dancers
and Custer memorabilia from Hardin; cattle drives and
cowboys in Miles City; miners in Butte.

I discovered the texture of Montana life from these
local histories, but the stories of early Montana I was most
drawn to came from another shelf. I loved to read anecdotes recorded on-the-spot in diaries and journals or
recalled in reminiscences. Even the self-mythologizing old
prostitute and adventurer, Calamity Jane, turns human
when an artful writer such as Teddy Blue Abbott—a real-
life cowboy—recalls an actual encounter in *We Pointed
Them North* (1939):

> *It was in 1907, and she was standing on a corner in
> Gilt Edge. . . . A few years before . . . some friends of
> hers had taken up a collection and sent her East to
> make a lady of her, and now she was back. I joked
> about her trip and asked her: "How'd you like
> it when they sent you East to get reformed and
> civilized?"*
>
> *Her eyes filled with tears. She said: "Blue, why
> don't the sons of bitches leave me alone and let me go
> to hell my own route: All I ask is to be allowed to live
> out the rest of my life with you boys who speak my
> language. And I hope they lay me beside Bill Hickok
> when I die."*

This aging Calamity, standing worn out and destitute on a street corner in Gilt Edge, is a different creature from the Wild West show caricature of popular fiction. You could run into an old derelict like her in your local bar. No matter where you live in the West, she is someone you might know.

When Granville Stuart does the telling in his multi-volume, self-justifying autobiography, *Forty Years on the Frontier* (1925), even a legendary shoot-out on Main Street appears sordid, accidental, and brutal:

> *Out in the street "Rattle Snake Jake" mounted his horse and Owen started to mount his, when he spied Joe Doney standing in front of Power's store. Revolver in hand he started to cross the street. When within a few feet of the walk Doney pulled a twenty-two caliber revolver and shot him in the stomach. A second shot struck Owen's hand, causing him to drop his revolver. . . .*
>
> *"Rattle Snake Jake," revolver in hand, started to ride up the street in the opposite direction, when a shot fired by someone in the saloon struck him in the side . . . and turning his horse he rode back to his comrade through a perfect shower of lead coming from both sides of the street and together the two men made their last stand in front of the tent [of photographer L. A. Huffman].*
>
> *When the smoke of battle cleared away examination of the bodies showed that "Rattle Snake Jake" had received nine wounds and Owen eleven, any one of which would have proved fatal.*

According to Stuart, Montana's first official historian, the dire crime for which these desperadoes paid with their lives was drinking and "cursing and swearing, declaring that they intended to clean up the town." So much for justice.

Justice. The very word is anathema to the Native American experience. In most popular westerns, the "Indian" is depicted as a noble savage or bloodthirsty savage —always savage in any account and as incomprehensible to "civilized" white folks as a cigar-store dummy. But to the old mountain man Andrew Garcia, Indians were people you lived with, friends and neighbors.

Dave and the kids and I drove up to Garcia's dilapidated homestead above Alberton. There were chickens, maybe a pig, some ratty horses in a broke-down corral. His kin lived there. It was real. In *Tough Trip through Paradise,* Garcia writes about getting lost in dense forests around Chief Joseph Pass with his Flathead wife, In-who-lise, called "Susie" for short. Their squabbles and strategies of love and revenge as they stumble over deadfalls and crash down rock slides are heartbreaking and funny. I loved this couple, knew only too well their domestic situation.

It delighted me to discover a shelf full of books that turned the western mythology on its head. One favorite is Frank Linderman's *Plenty-Coups, Chief of the Crows* (1930), in which I found a transcription of Plenty-Coups's anecdote, "Why I Do Not Like to Fight with White Men." By allowing white men to join his warriors, Plenty-Coups was trying to avoid trouble, to humor people who had destroyed his buffalo and were taking his land. But white men are simply too much trouble, he says, even when battling horse-stealing Blackfeet. White men wear too many clothes. They always want to eat. Their ineptness will endanger your war party. Plenty-Coups gets his revenge in this story, which politely yet scornfully denies their equality as humans, as warriors.

Almost every literate adventurer or settler knew she or he was involved in a venture of huge national importance and wrote a diary or journal to record participation in it. Out of this hodgepodge of experience and anecdote I found a few great voices that taught me how to tell stories. These storytellers led me to understand the place I had chosen to root myself in. The truth of a story, I discovered, lies in the teller.

One favorite is Emma Cowan, a ranch wife from the Gallatin Valley who wrote a reminiscence about going on a camping trip to Yellowstone Park in the summer of 1877 with her husband, her brother, and a group of friends. Emma's tale begins as a rather ordinary tourist story until Chief Joseph and his desperate band, on the run from the U. S. cavalry, burst in upon the Cowan's picnic. There would be mortal injury, captivity, and escape as a quiet day was invaded by history. But Emma's matter-of-fact voice fills the event with comedy.

A real storyteller creates a world alive with surprise, humor, pathos. He or she speaks in a voice as quirky and full of nuance as your own would be in your best dreams. Here, for instance, is Mary Ronan, in her reminiscence *Frontier Woman,* describing her girlhood in the gold-mining camp of Virginia City in 1863:

> *There were tall buttercups and blue flags in the valley. Up Alder Gulch snow and timber lilies bloomed, wild roses and syringa grew in sweet profusion and*

*flowering current bushes invited canaries to alight
and twitter. . . . On the tumbled hills among and over
which the town straggled the primroses made pink
splotches in early spring; there the yellow bells nodded and the bitterroots unfolded close to the ground
their perplexity of rose petals. . . . Robins, meadow-
larks, bluebirds, blackbirds, bluejays, crows and
magpies lured us from where men were ravishing
the gulch.*

And here is the schoolteacher voice of Thomas Dimsdale, writing about the same town in the same year in his
famous *Vigilantes of Montana.* He is talking about events
leading to the controversial hanging of one Captain J. A.
Slade:

*After the execution of the five men on the 14th of Jan-
uary the Vigilantes considered that their work was
nearly ended. They had freed the country from high-
waymen and murderers to a great extent, and they
determined that in the absence of the regular civil
authority they would establish a People's Court. . . .*
*J. A. Slade was himself, we have been informed,
a Vigilante; he openly boasted of it, and said he knew
all that they knew. . . . He and a couple of his depen-
dents might often be seen on one horse, galloping
through the streets, shouting and yelling, firing
revolvers, etc. On many occasions he would ride his
horse into stores; break up bars, toss the scales out of
doors, and use most insulting language to parties present. . . . For his wanton destruction of goods and furniture he was always ready to pay when sober if he*

*had money; but there were not a few who regarded
payment small satisfaction for the outrage, and these
were his personal enemies.*

Slade paid with his life. This is the mythological focus:
the outrage of righteous men becomes the violent law of the
West. Dimsdale's Virginia City is the one taught to school-
children and popularized in the media. I prefer Mary
Ronan's version. Men report battles; women report the intimate underside of life. More often than not their stories
deal with the complexities—the changing faces—of love.

In her reminiscence *A Bride Goes West* (1942), Nannie
Alderson moves through a series of emotional frontiers. It
was easy for an immigrant mother like me to identify with
her transformation from a Virginia belle to an enthusiastic
young ranch wife in Montana, to an isolated and anxious
mother, and finally to a self-sufficient widow. During the
course of her western initiation, Nannie encounters both
friendly and hostile Indians, sees her ranch house burned to
the ground, reports on her husband's shooting of the last
buffalo in the Tongue River country, gives birth to a child
alone on her kitchen table, and finally moves to Miles City
to run a boarding house.

Elizabeth Custer tells a different love story in *Boots
and Saddles* (1885), although here, too, I empathize with the
sadness, loneliness, and anxiety of frontier women—army
wives in this scenario, left behind the official parade when
their husbands marched off to war. As the women gathered at Fort Lincoln to sing and pray, their husbands were
being massacred by Sioux and Cheyenne warriors on a
grass-blown hillside in Montana, overlooking cottonwoods
and willows alongside the Little Big Horn River.

On Sunday afternoon, June 25, our little group of sad-
dened women, borne down with one common weight
of anxiety, sought solace in gathering together in our
house. We tried to find some slight surcease from trou-
ble in the old hymns; some of them dated back to our
childhood days, when our mothers rocked us to sleep
to their soothing strains. . . . All were absorbed in the
same thoughts, and their eyes were filled with faraway
visions and longings. Indescribable yearning for the
absent, and untold terror for their safety, engrossed
each heart. The words of the hymn,

> E'en though a cross it be
> Nearer, my God, to Thee

came forth with almost a sob from every throat.

Later I would read the account of a Cheyenne warrior,
Two Moons, telling the other side of the Custer story from
his vantage as a late-arriving participant in the battle. Two
Moons' tale is filled with pride and satisfaction but also
admiration for one white officer who fought valiantly, and
whose body was left untouched by the victorious Indian
women who mutilated the remains of his more cowardly
companions. This, too, although a warrior tale, in its complexity describes a fierce kind of love.

A most unlikely love story is cowboy Teddy Blue
Abbott's attachment to a handsome and brave young
Cheyenne warrior named Pine, who was unjustly accused
and jailed for an incident that started at Nannie Alderson's
place and led to the burning of her cabin. Abbott's relation-
ship, remembered in *We Pointed Them North*, crosses all
taboos and stereotypes:

*While they were all in jail, I went to see Pine every
day, and took him presents of tailor-made cigarettes
and candy and stuff. . . . The last day he took a silver
ring off his finger and gave it to me. The ring had a
little shield, and on the shield it said "C Co 7 Cav."
That was Tom Custer's company, and Pine took it off
the finger of one of Tom Custer's soldiers at the fight,
and he was in that fight when he was not yet fourteen
years old.*

Strange how these stories intertwine and circle one
another. Nannie Alderson, Teddy Blue Abbott, Tom
Custer, Elizabeth Custer, and two Cheyennes named Pine
and Two Moons. Not so strange when you realize there
were only a few hundred white people in Montana before
railroads brought hordes of land-hungry settlers. I know
a minister's wife in Missoula whose first husband was
Nannie Alderson's grandson. My friend's daughter went to
school with my twins, she married an Australian cowboy,
and this summer her first child was born on Nannie's old
homestead. Even today Montanans describe the state as one
neighborly town with six hundred-mile streets. We know
each other. We are connected. Because the landscape is so
huge, the human figures that inhabit it stand strong in
relief.

◘   ◘   ◘

One of the first friends I made in Montana was Vic Charlo,
son of the titular chief of the Flathead tribe. He had recently
dropped out of a Catholic seminary and become a student of
poetry. Vic took Dave and me and the poet Dick Hugo to

Good Friday services at the brick cathedral in the mission town of Saint Ignatius. Under frescoes painted by Italian monks a century before, we heard Flathead elders wailing the hymns and prayers in Salish. Later we drank together at the Milltown Bar; and still later became political accomplices in the War Against Poverty during the 1970s.

The literature of Montana is filled with relationships among whites and Indians, ordinary people trying to come to terms with their consciences. I should not have been surprised at Teddy Blue Abbott's moral stance — a sensitive cowboy writing about the injustice he will no longer have any part of. There were many sensitive writers who followed in Abbott's moral tracks: Joseph Kinsey Howard, Wallace Stegner, Dorothy Johnson, A. B. Guthrie, Jr., K. Ross Toole. But in Abbott's day there were not so many.

About the same time Teddy Blue drove cows from Texas to Miles City, another bright young man — the adventurer and Indian trader James Willard Schultz — took a Blackfeet girl as his bride. Schultz set up camp with the free Blackfeet near the Canadian border at the edge of the Rocky Mountain Front. In his first book of remembrances, *My Life as an Indian,* he wrote about his union with wry tenderness in a chapter called, "I Have a Lodge of My Own." Life was good, and full of promise. But Schultz did not stay with the Blackfeet through their ordeals and the loss of their freedom. He returned East to a proper marriage.

Schultz remained faithful in his heart to the companions of his youth. He returned years later to visit the Blackfeet on their reservation. Everything had changed. His friends and their families were dying of small pox and starvation. The U. S. government washed its hands of any responsibility to abet the "Starvation Winter" of 1883-84.

64

Schultz wrote furious letters to Congressmen and bureaucrats, and he finally got some food sent to the reservation. In the long meantime, many Blackfeet starved. The voice we hear in his later book, *Blackfeet and Buffalo,* is filled with disillusion. In the few years between James Willard's adolescence and maturity, a way of life eons older than America's Anglo history had been nearly wiped out.

I identified with Indians before I came to Montana, and afterward even more. I was dark and foreign and not Christian, and my people had been victims of genocide. I attached myself to nature and wild animals rather than to agriculture and cattle. And I loved the art, music, and spirit of Native Americans, all life connected in non-exploitive ways to forces of nature.

I wondered what the native people of Montana had to say about their story of dispossession. In Frank Linderman's book-length translations of the memories of Crow chief Plenty Coups and the old medicine woman Pretty Shield, there was a tragic progression. In youth they greeted whites with curiosity and trust, welcoming a powerful — yet equal — new people into a land full of buffalo and game, plenty for everyone. Pretty Shield's memories, like Plenty Coups's memories of the life before white contact, are Edenic. But then came war, death and knowledge and, by old age, despair — expulsion from the Garden. For unlike their Indian hosts, the whites were not interested in cohabitation. They had a different, exclusive notion of ownership and land. Pushed onto reservations, with the buffalo slaughtered, game hunted out, and tribes decimated by wars and disease, elders and chiefs spoke out in sad voices in transcribed treaty negotiations.

The "Flathead Railroad Treaty Negotiations of 1882"

and the "Proceedings of a Council with Sioux Indians of
Fort Peck Agency in 1886" read like contemporary one-act
plays, black tragicomedies in which the Indians try to outsmart the whites at their own game, playing out their hand
while knowing full well the deck is stacked against them.
In elaborate oratory, the Flathead chiefs asked millions for
the railroad right-of-way; they were forced to settle for fifteen thousand dollars. In the Sioux Proceedings the debate
was about work on a shrinking reservation populated by
hunter/warriors and governed by white agents appointed
in Washington. The Sioux argument centers on better
terms for assimilation. More mules and plows, potatoes
and wages.

The final step in the Native American oral literature
of loss goes beyond disillusionment to a fine bitter anger.
We hear it in the famous words that are ascribed to the
Nez Perce's Chief Joseph as he accepted defeat in the Bear
Paw Mountains: "I will fight no more forever." And we
hear it more vehemently in a speech attributed to my friend
Vic's great-grandfather, the Flatheads' Chief Charlot,
whose band was pushed out of his tribe's ancestral lands in
the Bitterroot by the treachery and lying of U. S. government officials. Outraged at the notion that his people
would have to pay taxes for that privilege, in "The Indian
and Taxation," Charlot says:

> *Yes, my people, the white man wants us to pay him.*
> *He comes in his intent, and says we must pay him —*
> *pay him for our own, for the things we have from our*
> *God and our forefathers; for things he never owned*
> *and never gave us. What law or right is that? What*
> *shame or what charity? . . .*

*And is he not foul? He has filled graves with our
bones. His horses, his cattle, his sheep, his men, his
women have rot. Do not his breath, his gums stink?
His jaws lose their teeth and he stamps them with
false ones, yet he is not ashamed. No, no! His course is
destruction; he spoils the Spirit who gave us this
country made beautiful and clean. But that is not
enough: he wants us to pay him, besides his enslaving
our country. Yes, and our people, besides, that degra-
dation of a tribe who never were his enemies . . .*

The battle for property did not end with conquest
of Indian lands. Soon poor, white outlaws were stealing
horses and running them over the Canadian border for sale.
They rustled cattle off the open range, hid in the rugged
canyons of the Missouri Breaks. A new, upper-crust vigilante system was organized to protect such movable property from riff-raff thieves. Its members included a president
(Teddy Roosevelt) and a nobleman (Marquis de Mores). As
in feudal days, the contest was between life and property,
with property ascendant. Granville Stuart, one of the vigilante group's prime movers, defends the winning side in
"Cattle Rustlers and Vigilantes," from his voluminous reminiscences, *Forty Years on the Frontier.* I wonder if Stuart's
corrupted vision is the history we should take to heart.

Fortunately, frontier life was often comic, and the
stories that give me most pleasure are salted and peppered
with a great deal of humor. Humor acted as a leavening
agent against work and poverty. In *Devil Man with a Gun*
(1967), Art H. Watson tells the hilarious tale of a mule-
skinner called, for obvious reasons, "Stuttering Shorty."
Imagine the predicament when Shorty's brakes fail, the

mules must be spoken to, and the skinner cannot speak!
Other humorous tales act as strategies for survival —
fireside warnings like John R. Barrows's "Circular Story,"
from *Ubet* (1935), his book about cowboy life in a small
town of that name. By the time I got to Ubet it had
changed its name to Garneil. Maybe a hundred people live
in the ramshackle hamlet at the foot of the Snowy Mountains, where we filmed the movie *Heartland*. There is Garneil, and East Garneil, a post office and a new cultural
center donated by *Heartland's* New York producer, Mike
Hausman. Mike fell in love with Montana. He bought a
ranch across from our main location, runs buffalo on it,
and named his son Colt. You need a sense of humor to survive in Garneil.

The most famous western humorist of Montana's
cowboy frontier days was artist and tall-tale-teller, Charles
M. Russell. Here is a voice that is self-consciously partici-
pating in the western myth, but the participation is alto-
gether self-mocking. In "The Story of a Cowpuncher,"
from his posthumously published book of yarns, *Trails
Plowed Under* (1937), Russell's cowpoke persona, Rawhide
Rawlins, sizes up the situation:

> *"Speakin' of cowpunchers," says Rawhide Rawlins,
> "I'm glad to see in the last few years that them that
> knows about the business have been writin' about
> 'em. It begins to look like they'd be wiped out without
> a history. Up to a few years ago there's mighty little
> known about cows and cow people. It was sure
> amusin' to read some of them old stories about cow-
> punchin'. You'd think a puncher growed horns an'
> was haired over.*

*"It put me in mind of the eastern girl that asks
her mother: 'Ma,' says she, 'Do cowboys eat grass?'
'No dear,' says the old lady, 'they're part human,' an'
I don't know but the old gal had 'em sized up right."*

Which brings me full circle to the mythological Montana of pulp westerns. Yes, there were cowboys, outlaws, vigilantes, pioneers. And six million bison, and fierce Indians in eagle feathers. But I found a different reality in the basement stacks as I browsed through my free afternoons. The stories I found are more complex than the six-gun myth, richer in particularities. Filled with the ambiguities of conquest and colonialism, they form a literature I can live inside of. When legends fail we must rely on stories that tell the truth.

Law of the Range

Git along little dogies
I'm leavin Cheyenne,
Gone to Montana
To throw the Houlihan

TRADITIONAL COWBOY BALLAD

When we first came to Montana, Dave and I went to horse
and cattle auctions in Missoula. We bought boots and
Stetson hats, horses and as much tack as we could afford,
which wasn't much. We took the kids to rodeos, tried to
involve them in our dream of the West, which came from
a lifetime of reading classic westerns, tapping our heels to
too many country-and-western songs on the radio, being
addicted to Wild West movies.

Soon we were to meet real cowmen, like our rancher
neighbors, father Ernest and son Sidney Wills, old-time
Montanans whose family has leased our meadow for summer cattle pasture these twenty-two years. Fixing fence,
driving cows out of hayfields, cutting and stacking hay, trying to nurse injured horses larger and stronger than both of
us combined, were healthy and sweaty antidotes to our
romanticism.

My investigation into the real life of Montana continued and accelerated after Dave died. I found another true

companion in Bill Kittredge, a writer and teacher who had
grown up on a huge ranch on eastern Oregon's high desert
and knew the buckaroo life from the inside out. Together
we embarked on a study of western history and folk culture that has kept me on the road and inquisitive from the
Canadian Rockies to Bisbee, Arizona, from Burns, Oregon,
to Pawhuska, Oklahoma.

The original fascination with the West that landed
me in Montana is still alive and kicking. It has led me to
specialize in such arcane knowledge as the makeup of
grasslands and lava beds, the lives of hermit women, and
the work of men who enforce the not-so-glamorous laws
of the range.

C   C   C

Less than two hundred years ago the Great Plains were
rich with wild grasses. Thirty million bison grew fat on
that grass. In George Catlin's paintings from the 1860s, we
see lime-green hills striped and dotted with humped beasts.
In "Herd on the Move," William J. Hays paints a V-shaped
swarm, brown to the horizon. Indians, nomadic as their
prey, hunted the bison and lived in plentitude. The grass
renewed life.

"Then," wrote L. A. Huffman, Montana's premiere
frontier photographer, "came the cattlemen, the 'trail boss'
and his army of cowboys, and the great cattle roundups.
Then the army of railroad builders. That—the railway—
was the fatal coming." Huffman's vision is clouded with
cheap regret and nostalgia. "One looked about and said,
'This is the last West.'"

The so-called cattlemen's frontier ended with the

cow-killing winters of the 1880s as much as it ended with the railroads, the rush of homesteaders, and the breakup of the open range. It ended when high-plains ranchers discovered they would have to feed cattle. They would have to become farmers. Barbed wire went up; people shot each other over water rights; wandering ruffians — buffalo hunters, wolfers, woodcutters, trappers — were hard-pressed to find a living off the depleted and tamed land.

"The rustlers of that day were a different class of men from the sneak thieves of today," wrote Teddy Blue Abbott in his cowboy classic, *We Pointed Them North.* "They went in armed bands, took what they wanted by force, and defied arrest. It come to a showdown, fight or quit. . . ."

Cattle barons such as Granville Stuart banded together to take law into their own hands (even Teddy Roosevelt was implicated in Stuart's infamous vigilante group, the 'Stranglers'). "It had come to be almost impossible to keep a team or saddle horse on a ranch unless one slept in the manger with a rifle," said Stuart.

Some ranchers claimed that up to three percent of their cattle was lost to rustlers who hid out in the rough Missouri Breaks of eastern Montana. In July of 1884 Stuart's vigilantes hung a dozen men. Some folks were not so sure about Stuart's motives. "Friends of the rustlers . . . ," wrote Teddy Blue, "circulated stories that he had killed poor settlers in order to clear them off the range and have more room for his cattle."

Brands are an ancient means for declaring ownership. The one we designed when we bought our land, but have almost never used, is the 6S, meaning "This animal belongs to the Six Smiths."

Nearly four thousand years ago Egyptian herders stamped brands on their cows. When Hernando Cortez stepped off his vessel on the gulf coast of Mexico, the conquistadors unloaded six heifers and a bull, all branded with three small crosses. Meriwether Lewis branded his equipment when he cached it along the route of the Lewis and Clark expedition to the Pacific in 1805 and 1806.

The first stockmen's association was formed in Colorado in 1867, primarily to register brands and so discourage rustlers. I belong to the Bonita/Greenough/Clinton/Potomac Cattlemen's Association—a privilege that came with the deed to our land. One of the earliest laws passed by Montana's Territorial Legislature in 1864 required registration of brands. And in 1885, in the wake of arbitrary revenge-seeking by vigilantes, the Montana legislature created a Board of Stock Commissioners to hire brand inspectors and range detectives. Protection of property on the hoof became an obligation of the state. Granville Stuart described the duties of inspectors:

> *All stock . . . should be inspected by the employees of the Stock Commissioners before it could be driven or shipped out. All persons driving or shipping any stock out of the territory were compelled to give the inspectors a receipt for all stock not carrying their brand. This stock could then be taken to eastern markets and sold. . . . The money received had to be turned over to the Board of Stock Commissioners and was by them distributed to the real owners.*

The system worked. In 1886, 83,991 Montana cattle were inspected in stockyards with the recovery of 1,659 strays; an additional 459 strays were recovered on the range. Inspectors saved ranchers thousands of dollars, and the deputized stock detectives arrested forty-three thieves.

But the law of the range was not always rational. You might have bad men chasing good folks. Maybe inspired by the earlier successes of their Montana brethren, in 1892 Wyoming cattlemen hired mercenaries to gun down "suspected rustlers"—a code name for immigrant homesteaders—in the myth-making Johnson County Wars (*Shane, Heaven's Gate*).

Or you had bad men chasing bad men. Take Tom Horn. In 1894, impatient with short jail sentences and small fines for convicted cattle rustlers, a few of the most avid ranchers in the Wyoming Stock Growers Association secretly hired Horn, an ex-Indian scout turned Pinkerton investigator, to clean out rustlers in southern Wyoming. They offered a bounty—dead or alive.

"Killing men is my specialty," Horn bragged. "I look at it as a business proposition, and I think I have a corner on the market."

In this case, as in so many instances of showdown violence, the solution was worse than the problem. One of the victims Horn got paid to kill was a fourteen-year-old boy. You might call Tom Horn a fatal coming.

There have been many 'fatal comings' on the northern plains since Huffman's lament (most fatal was the internal combustion engine). What Huffman regretted was the passing of a way of life—certainly not the only or the best. Ask any Native American. Life changes. There can be no "last West."

◼   ◼   ◼

The range detectives and brand inspectors I have met or
read about have no myth to honor them. They came of age
during the Great Depression and their collective story fills
a blank spot in the history books. It takes place horseback
and in pickups on back roads and snowbound ranches; it
reeks of the stockyards in Chicago, Omaha, Denver, St.
Paul. You hear in the voices of such men the small-town
twang of Montana, Idaho, Colorado, Wyoming, Nebraska,
the Dakotas. Earl Haller, from Loma, Colorado, slouches
astride his favorite roping horse. "I'm just a common guy
I guess—raised up poor and I'm still poor."

Go to a cattle sale in a western town and you will see
these old-timers trading stories. They know everyone.
That's part of the job: being gregarious, knowing the
people in a ranching community as well as they know the
cattle and the land. Say a rancher has discovered some
stranger's cows in his fall roundup. The brand inspector
will come out to the pens, he will clip the hide clean around
the brand, and he will be expected to identify the owner.

The inspector may stay for a cup of coffee, chew the
fat with the wife, trade gossip. This is the life he was bred
to. Most range detectives and brand inspectors were raised
on small family ranches. Their parents and grandparents
came west in covered wagons or drove cattle north from
Texas and stayed to claim a small homestead. One I know
of came from Liverpool; another from Switzerland.

Lee Sackett was born in 1914 on the north fork of
Wyoming's Powder River. His uncles broke horses for an
Englishman named Malcolm Moncreef, who shipped the
horses from the Big Horns to England, for the cavalry.
Sackett grew up on a 160-acre homestead just north of
Hole in the Wall. "When it was good," says Lee, "it was

tough. When it was bad, it was some of the worst country in the world."

Howard Harmon's grandfather was one of the "Badland Cowboys" who rode with A. C. Huidekeper's famous horse-ranching outfit in North Dakota. His mother's uncle was killed in Wyoming's Johnson County War. Bob Fitch, from Rifle, Colorado, has a photo of himself as a child, riding with Teddy Roosevelt on a bear hunt. On "Bus" Farnum's wall is a faded L. A. Huffman photograph of his family's ranch on Cottonwood Creek.

When the home ranch failed, or was taken over by an older brother, these men would cowboy for a larger outfit. They knew the ways of cattle, loved horses, and were decent ropers. Almost all of them rodeoed when they were bucks. A few are still competing. At eighty, Floyd Hicks from Lewistown, Montana, won the old-timers roping competition at Broadus. At eighty-two he broke two fingers at a jackpot rodeo. He's a tough one. "The doctor talked me into cutting them off," he says with a shrug.

Hicks was born in 1905 in the Sweetgrass Hills near Whitlash, Montana, with an Indian servant as midwife. At six he would pass Charlie Russell's studio on his four-mile trek to school. On clear, cold nights wolves attacked horses in his father's corral; he remembers horses screaming. There was no electricity or cars or telephones. When Hicks went to work as a state brand inspector in 1926, he was sent to the Chicago stockyards. "That Capone beer was good beer," he says. "Chicago was my college education."

Some brand inspectors were top hands for big ranchers and turned to their new trade in retirement. Others followed their fathers into the business. Most have knocked around, working in oil fields, on railroad gangs, hard-rock

mining. They worked in sale barns and auctions, sometimes in law enforcement. Nearly every one of them knew
hard times during the Depression, saw action in the armed
services in World War II, and witnessed the mechanical
revolutions of the post-war era—men and horses replaced
by tractors, pickups, horse trailers, and semis.

These men are old now. As young cowhands they saw
the small ranches of the northern plains consolidated in
agribusiness and tamed to mechanization, and found
themselves adrift—a nearly extinct breed, without jobs
or futures. It wasn't a big leap for an ambitious cowboy
to become a brand inspector. Instead of one boss, he
would have many—cattlemen's associations or state gov-
ernments—yet he still served the ruling-class ranchers,
protected their property.

Orlin Corn, from Grand Junction, Colorado, was a
brand inspector in the Denver stockyards. "Title to billions
of dollars throughout the West," he says, "is determined by
the brands on livestock." Herb Callen sums it up: "A person
always wants to remember you're working for the ranchers
because they're the ones who are actually paying you."

The job didn't pay much to begin with, but it was sure
better than a Depression cowboy's wages of room and
board and, say, thirty-five dollars a month. In 1944 Bob
Fitch received "125 dollars a month and six cents per mile."
He jumped at the opportunity. This was a profession you
could get ahead in. You didn't have to ride the grub line or
the freight trains. You could get married and raise a family
and save up for your own piece of ground. If you worked
for the state, you could retire with a pension.

A brand inspector or range detective had to have a
good visual memory, to know the brands of all the ranches

in his region. He had to recognize brands on milling cattle in a sale yard. He would know the ways of fakery.

When Montana cattleman Wellington Rankin reported wide-scale rustling in the 1960s, chief investigator L. C. Johnston (grandson of mountain man "Liver Eatin' Johnson") found his suspect by remembering a brand. A Holstein dairy farmer named Bruce Johnson, whose land bordered Rankin's, had registered the backward BK brand. Rankin's brand was EY. A few touches with a branding iron and EY becomes BK. The investigator, in the guise of a B. L. M. agent, checked out the suspect's corrals when the cattle were gathered to be shipped off that fall.

"Christ, a blind man could read the fresh worked-over brands," says L. C. He discovered 156 cows and 140 calves that had been stolen—the largest cattle heist in recent history. There was a showdown with guns. The bandit went off to the pen in Deer Lodge for twenty-five years, but got free in two and a half. "The son of a bitch claimed he had emphysema," snorts L. C. Johnston.

As the cattle industry changed, so did the work of brand inspectors and range detectives. Hauling cattle to feedlots in semitrailers replaced railroads, as railroads had replaced the long cattle drives. Modern rustlers often butcher on the spot and pack the meat into a Cadillac trunk; or they load stock into goose-neck trailers and ride the freeways across state lines before anyone knows the cattle are gone. It's nearly impossible to track down such thievery.

In 1889 about 8,000 brands had been recorded in Montana. Today there are 57,000. A sophisticated computer system keeps the lists up-to-date. Brand inspection has become a big-time government activity. Montana has a seven-person Board of Livestock, a staff of eighteen district or field inspectors, and seventeen market inspectors. There are similar institutions in other western cattle-producing states.

"Now no one takes pride in their work," says Joe Bowman, a retired district supervisor from the South Platte country near Brush, Colorado. He has bridged the transition from vigilantes to computers. "There's no loyalty, just a paycheck."

With computerized brands and piles of paperwork, the duties have become increasingly bureaucratic. Bud Corder, from Butte, says, "You used to have to be a cowboy to be a Brand Inspector. If you're a bookkeeper you have a better shot at it now."

　　 ⊏　　⊏　　⊏

Besides low wages and back-breaking labor, the job could be thankless in other ways. Cowboys who became brand inspectors were often distrusted by their own kind and disdained by the ranchers they served; it was their duty to snitch. Before superhighways made rustling a road sport, most small-time thievery was done on horseback by the hired hands of outfits that ran thousands of mother cows over miles of grazing lands. You could siphon off three or four unbranded calves, say they were lost to coyotes, and start your own herd. It was one of the few bonuses a cowhand could expect. A range detective might go undercover for the county sheriff, working as a hired hand on a ranch with rustling problems. Fritz Bartley, from Hygiene, Colorado, carried on such a pretense for nine years. "I'll bet I punched more cattle than most inspectors," says Fritz. The range detective might discover rustlers in the nest and then see them walk free because the owners didn't want to prosecute. Maybe the hand was worth more than the cows. Maybe the rustler was the rancher's son.

Joe Bowman says, "There's always been petty rustling." A smile trickles across his wide lips. "One guy's son was selling his dad's cattle to buy whiskey. I knew about it, but the son was going into the army in six weeks to fight in World War II. So I left him alone, and when he came back he was straight and ran his dad's ranch. That was better than breaking his parents' hearts and ruining him in prison."

A familiar shrug accompanies such words. Read the shrug as an ironic notion of justice. These old-time lawmen of the range are tough and stoic as goats. Work has made them hard-handed, stove-up, laconic. They have birthed calves, fed cattle in blizzards, butchered the cows they nurtured in the necessary blood-and-guts slaughter that transforms living animals into meat. You will find no soft sentimentality in them, yet they adhere to a code tempered by individual judgment, wise in the ways of human frailty and possibilities for redemption.

Unlike a new generation of land- and stock-watching bureaucrats, these old cowboys know some things you do not learn in college. Not one of them holds a B.S. degree from an agricultural institution, and most never finished high school. They were schooled in the ways of wind and grazing ungulates. They will be buried under prairie grass. In our myth of America, the cowboy rides the big lonesome and sings to cows. These old range-riders are among the self-chosen few who adhere to the reality under the mythic gloss. They know what it takes to survive in an unforgiving place without losing their humanity or their humor.

"I don't want to be a hero," says Bill Apple, a retired
inspector who claims to be the first white man born on
Bone Pile Creek, south of Gillette, Wyoming. That was in
1911, when Indians camped at neighboring Caballo Creek
and "the whole country was open." Bill studies a photographic likeness of himself as if the man in the Stetson is a
stranger. "It's a hard-looking guy in there," he says, "but it
must be me."

White collars may rule at the top, but it's guys like Bill
Apple who carry on in the traditional ways. Our electronic,
mechanized culture has distanced us from the sources of
life. We yearn to fish in clear waters, to walk in pristine
mountains, but we refuse to dirty our hands.

◘   ◘   ◘

After a reading I gave with Bill Kittredge at the University
of Colorado a couple of years ago, I met a Denver photographer, Stephen Collector, whose obsession was tracking
down and photographing old-time range detectives and
brand inspectors. Collector was following in the tradition
of L. A. Huffman and Edward Sheriff Curtis, who
believed they could preserve a vision of the West through
images in black and white.

"The passing of every old man or woman," said Curtis
in 1907, in defense of his *North American Indian* collection,
"means the passing of some tradition, some knowledge of
sacred rites possessed by no other. . . . The information that
is to be gathered for the benefit of future generations . . .
must be collected at once or the opportunity will be lost for
all time."

Collector began with a portrait of Lyman Edgar, taken

in 1979 at the sale barn in La Junta, Colorado. "I looked for some vestige of the romance and adventure of Bent's Fort," says Collector. "But what I saw was the business side of cowboying. There was nothing romantic about a guy working the stock pens."

The light was harsh; the September air was hot and dry; the feedlot stink was overpowering. Collector had serious doubts, but "soon came a bandy-legged sixty-five-year-old cowboy wearing sunglasses and a battered black Stetson. Soon afterward the light didn't look so bad. . . . Now as I travel the West," he continues, "it is these faces I see and remember. They bring life to the vast spaces."

I can't help but agree. Seeing life in vast spaces—particular, detailed life in sharp focus—is what we lovers of the West love most. We want to write stories, carve sculptures, take pictures of old men who lean against barns at stock auctions, ride the white horse leading the rodeo parade.

Our old men squint into the light with small hard eyes. We know they have scraped cowshit off their polished go-to-town boots. Their names are turn-of-the-century Anglo, German, Scandinavian names you find in obituaries from every western hamlet. In such names we recognize a dominant strain in the white man's settlement of the plains. These are the grandfathers and bachelors who die unnoticed in old-people's homes.

The old men loom large against a background of faraway mountains. The Tetons, the Big Horns, the Missions. Or a sweep of grass, or wheat, or the mud-brown South Platte, high with spring run-off, glinting beyond sagebrush. I imagine hoot owls, the dissonant cries of red-winged blackbirds in the tules.

On a sand-blasted log wall in my living room, I have hung Stephen Collector's photograph of Richard "Buster" Priddy next to portraits of Dick Hugo and my father's best friend, Nelson Algren. I imagine conversations among these three cantankerous old men, and it gives me heart, makes me laugh when I feel most alone or weak.

Buster Priddy was eighty-four when his picture was taken, and he was still working as a stock inspector from his homestead ranch near Dixon, Montana. His Irish father, an itinerant plasterer and gambler, had drifted into the Great Falls area just after the turn of the century. "I'd have to go to the Mint or the Silver Dollar or the Milwaukee Bar to get him, scared he'd knock the shit out of me," said Priddy. "I knew every ash can and alley in Great Falls."

Sweat has stained a band around Buster's shapeless Stetson. His mouth is set in a hard, straight line — no teeth. At twelve Priddy quit school to build roads with horse teams. He ran wild horses and traded them; ranched; served as deputy sheriff out of Thompson Falls for twenty years. He and his wife of sixty-three years live in separate houses on their small ranch. "It works out better that way," says the old buzzard.

Here is where Hugo or Algren might guffaw, might interrupt with a similar story. They knew nothing about brand inspectors or range detectives, but they had spent hours, weeks, months in cowboy bars, milltown bars, mining town bars; and they'd seen Buster's face all over the West. He is a western everyman.

Horseback traditions are dying with men of Buster's generation — a code of the cattleman's frontier that was dying before Buster was born. But agriculture continues, and new immigrants keep coming West, and it is good to remind ourselves of the personal ties that bind men like Buster to land, to animals, often to women, always to each other. They are deeply planted. We care about Buster and his cohorts because we have come to understand that the history of place is most often found in ordinary lives. To survive with any grace, we must take lessons from old men in blue denim.

The River That Runs Through It

On summer evenings I look north from the deck outside
my log kitchen and watch night crawl up the Bear Creek
drainage from the blue-black valley of the Big Blackfoot.
I cannot see the river or the creek from where I sit, but the
humped mountains all around are scarred by clear-cuts and
slashed with logging roads. Owls cry. Ghosts of old forests
rise in dusky light. I imagine the deep woods as they were
before Anaconda, before Champion and Plum Creek. A
long-billed snipe dives from the clouds, wind sounding
through his feathers in a trilling, whistling mating call.

Some nights the northern sky pulses green — green
waves and luminous stripes passing over the eaves of my
shake roof. After fireworks one Fourth of July in our
Wild-West days of the 1970s, a bunch of good old boys and
gals were passing the Jack Daniel's around a fire burned
down to coals. A visiting writer stood by the tailgate of his
pickup, stoned on acid. He looked up to the sky, then at us.
"You seeing the same thing I am?"

I cannot fathom what my friend saw in his altered
state, but the rest of us were craning our heads toward
the light show on the Milky Way. We studied the northern
lights with the fascination of Neanderthals gawking
outside their caves. Remembering that night I think of

light flowing like a river; I think of blood and sap—the common, recurrent, and fluid patterns of life.

ᴇ　ᴇ　ᴇ

I am not a fisherperson. I have tried many times to catch fish on a line—sometimes to please others, sometimes to satisfy myself—but I do not like to snap the necks of shiny, wiggling cutthroat trout or rainbows or Dolly Vardens. "You eat them, you can kill them," Dave would scold me.

Where I live you learn that respectful tracking and killing of wild game is more honest than buying domestic meat—better for the world, perhaps better for the soul. Killing, however, is never a matter of logic. My squeamishness regarding fish goes back to my Chicago childhood. My fat little Grandma Deutch would take me to the Jewish fishmonger's shop on Broadway for smoked Lake Michigan whitefish in wax paper: smelly, greasy, but delicious when sautéed in butter. And after thunderstorms at our summer house in the Michigan dunes, scores of alewives would float onto the beach and die, their stink so rotten we held our noses. Still, I attach myself to men who love to fish. And it has been my good fortune to live along trout streams.

When my young family came to Montana in the fall of 1964, we spent our first day fishing Rock Creek, a blue-ribbon stream in the Clark Fork's drainage. Dick Hugo took us. He had convinced Dave to leave Seattle and join the English Department at the University of Montana. We could have looked for houses to rent, checked out the university where Dave would teach on Monday. "Let's go fishing," said Dave.

The River That Runs Through It

Dave and Dick and our eldest son, Eric, fished the
narrow canyon while I untangled six-year-old Steve's line.
Yellow aspen and cottonwoods speckled the creek bottoms,
and the valley was streaked red with vine maple. Ponderosa pines, western larch, and Douglas fir fringed the
burnt-grass hillsides. God or nature, certainly not accident,
had endowed the land with the same colors and markings
as the trout.

We spent every off-day fishing Rock Creek, and
within a year we had rented a streamside bungalow at the
Valley of the Moon Ranch. I was still in my twenties, only
a few years removed from the innocence of childhood.
That was before our twins were born, before my black hair
turned gray, before David realized he had a fatal heart
disease.

But those were the Rock Creek years, and they are
not part of this story. This story begins six years later and is
about my family and neighbors, a way of life, a book, and
a river named the Big Blackfoot to distinguish it from the
Little Blackfoot.

In western Montana, all highways run along pine-
forested river routes carved through mountains by ice and
running water. The Big Blackfoot empties into the Clark
Fork of the Columbia River a few miles east of Missoula.
Our place sits on a meadow a mile and a half above the
Blackfoot, but the river's presence ripples in my imagination as if it murmured outside my door. The Big Blackfoot
has become my metaphor for change and connection. It
seems I have been standing in the same place for a quarter
century, watching the chaos of my life flow by.

There is an idyllic morning I carry around with me
like a lucky rubbing stone. It is 1971, our first summer at

the ranch, and Dave and I and our four boys have gone
fishing on the Big Blackfoot. We drive our sand-colored
Land Rover to the edge of a high bank upstream from the
mouth of Belmont Creek. Dave and the older boys scramble down to the rocky shore. It is cool in the morning shade
of great-branched Ponderosas. The salmon-fly hatch is
about over, but a few of the heavy, orange-bodied insects
hang onto willow branches in the dewy air. When their
wings dry, they will beat suicidally over riffles where
lunker rainbows are waiting for breakfast.

"Use live ones for bait," shouts Dave, knee-deep in
green water. Dave moves toward the head of a fishing hole.
The boys and I hop through willows, serviceberry and
chokecherry brush. We snatch the sluggish salmon flies.
Within the hour Dave hooks and nets two twenty-inch
rainbows. Eric and Steve with their squiggling live flies
catch smaller trout. Even I get a good bite. The fishing is
hot, and then it's over.

I bring out tuna-fish sandwiches, peaches, and
chocolate-chip cookies. A thermos of coffee. A jar of
lemonade. After lunch, with the sun high and the water
cool, I am happy to lie on damp sand, the older guys
gone downriver in search of elusive big ones, the four-
year-old twins making dams out of colored river stones—
aquamarine, rose, jade green.

Norman Maclean would soon memorialize such Pre-
cambrian "rocks from the basement of time" in the title
story of *A River Runs Through It*. He would describe the
Big Blackfoot's deep patterns: the unity of a three-part fishing hole, the river's billion-year geologic history. Maclean
would connect the river and the act of fishing to a Presbyterian brand of theology and to an aesthetic of craft and art.

He would articulate universal feelings of helplessness in the face of destiny and death.

But on that faraway summer morning I had no idea that my humanities professor from the University of Chicago lived just up the road at Seeley Lake. I did not know his wife had recently died or that he had retired from teaching. I would never have guessed that twenty miles upriver, at the age of seventy-three, Norman Maclean was beginning to write a great book about family and fishing and love. Or that the book's culminating scene would take place exactly where I sat, daydreaming in the midday Blackfoot breeze.

◧   ◧   ◧

My husband Dave grew up along the Mississippi in Hastings, Minnesota, and loved to skate. He read the boys *Hans Brinker and the Silver Skates* so they would get the idea of his life on the river. "We'd skate the backwaters," he said. "Make fires, tease the girls." His words created a Brueghel world, a nostalgic etching by Currier & Ives.

In winter, at our favorite swimming hole a quarter mile above the mouth of Bear Creek, the Blackfoot freezes two feet thick and two-thirds of the way to its northern shore. Twenty yards downstream the riffles run year around. The beach we call ours is a gravel pocket bounded by high cliffs embroidered orange and chartreuse with lichen. I have skied down to the river in January, played tag on the ice with little boys and puppies, followed tracks of deer, rabbits, and mice.

We never skated on Blackfoot pools because there was too much snow those winters of the early seventies, snow four feet deep in our field. And Dave was too ill to skate. Disease had caused his arteries to become clogged with the yellow cholesterol we could see in patches under his deep-circled blue eyes. Dave did not have the energy to clear an ice rink on the river, and I didn't care enough to do it myself.

"I want Annick and the kids to have something after I'm gone," Dave told our dear friend, Anne Stadler, knowing he could die any day. The hundred-year-old hewn-log house we found abandoned along the Blackfoot, then tore apart and rebuilt on our 163 acres would be his hedge against mortality. But Dave had other reasons for wanting to own land. He had grown up poor and illegitimate, bearing the name of his mother's family, and he wanted the respectability of property with his name on the deed.

I have come to realize he also wanted to cheat fear and fate by living out fantasies of his rural childhood. "What do you want to be when you grow up?" our oldest boy, Eric, would ask his father. The question was a joke because Dave changed professions the way other restless men change wives. First he had been a lawyer, then an English professor, finally an aspiring filmmaker. Dave's answer became a family catchword: "I want to be a cowboy."

The Blackfoot Valley offered a haven where the Cowboy could fish, hunt birds, ride his horses, and own land wild enough to harbor elk, deer, mountain lions, and black bear. My dreams of escape joined easily with his, and I became the Ranch Wife. Land lasts longer than blood or love. It is not like a river.

◧   ◧   ◧

After Dave's death in 1974, I spent two years in Spokane producing a series of documentaries about Native Americans. We drove to Seattle those years for Christmas holidays with the Stadlers. By 1976 we were healed enough to celebrate Christmas at home. I was back in the Blackfoot Valley and editing a new film about Dick Hugo, a film that incorporated parts of the original Dave and I had made ten years earlier. I had become the self-starter Dave always wanted me to be, a liberated widow forty years old, but I was still tied to my grief. I slept with Dave's pajamas, the scent of him, under my pillow.

Eric and Steve had come home from college. The twins, Alex and Andrew, who were in fourth grade at the Potomac School, tore into the presents under the tree. We feasted on ham scored with mustard and brown sugar, then gathered around the red brick fireplace that I had designed and Steve had helped build. It was our first addition to the house since Dave died, and we knew he would be proud of us for creating a beautiful handmade thing.

We sat around the crackling fire, played word games, listened to the scratched recording of Dylan Thomas reading "A Child's Christmas in Wales" that Dave had given me for my eighteenth birthday. We did our best to drive off melancholy. There was a book I had intended to give to Eric or Steve as a present, but once I started reading it, I could not let it go. The slim volume had a powder blue dust jacket. It was the first edition of *A River Runs Through It*.

"Your father would have loved this book," I told the boys.

I read the ending aloud. *Eventually, all things merge into one, and a river runs through it. . . .*

Seven years later, in September of 1983, Norman

Maclean inscribed my dog-eared copy: "To Annick Smith
—Who lives where it is more beautiful but so tough the
Finns and the Serbs lined their fields with rock-piles and
then gave up." We had become partners—Norman, Bill
Kittredge, and me—in the development of a dramatic film
based on that book.

The day Maclean signed my book I had gone to pick
him up at his cabin on Seeley Lake. The lake is fed by the
Clearwater River, which is a tributary to the Big Blackfoot
and part of the same fierce snow country. Five-hundred-
year-old larch climb from the shore, and each fall the larch
shed golden needles on the shingle roof of the log cabin
that Norman helped his father build in 1922. When I
arrived I was shocked to see the eighty-five-year-old author
descending a ladder from the roof, broom in hand.

"You should take care!" I admonished.

"I *am* taking care," Norman snapped back at me.

We walked to his dock and gazed across the lake to a
peak in the Swan Range Wilderness, where a forest fire
burned unchecked. Norman worked for the Forest Service
in the Bitterroot Mountains as a young man and had come
to detest its cut-down-the-trees-and-make-money politics.
His last book, *Young Men and Fire,* was about the Mann
Gulch fire of 1948, where thirteen young smoke-jumpers
died senselessly. He was concerned to the end about taking
care of what you love.

Eventually Bill wrote a script for *A River Runs
Through It* under Norman's exacting tutelage, and I began
the long and painful process of raising production money.
But Norman became ill and Robert Redford became interested in directing and producing the film, and Norman
sold him the rights because he believed that in Redford's

hands the film would be made soon and made right. The result was a new script by a professional screenwriter and an Academy Award-winning movie that Norman did not live to see.

The final irony of *A River Runs Through It* is that the film was not shot on the Big Blackfoot. If any story is wedded to place, that one is, but logged-off hillsides make disturbing pictures. The river had become too degraded for Redford's idyllic vision.

◧　◧　◧

The Big Blackfoot is degraded. It is number twelve in the nation on the American Rivers Group's 1994 listing of threatened watersheds. Above Lincoln, the Blackfoot's upper reaches are barren, poisoned by arsenic and other hard metals leached into the waters from a century of mining for gold, silver, and other precious metals. The area has become one of Montana's beleaguered Superfund sites, with lawsuits and studies and cleanup beginning but having no end in sight.

The mining danger is far from over. Phelps Dodge and Canyon Resources are planning an immense cyanide heap-leach gold-mining operation upstream from the Lander's Fork that will run along the Blackfoot for over a mile. The company intends to dig a pit 1200 feet deep — 700 feet below groundwater level. They plan to stack the 400 million tons of rock from their pit along Highway 200, adjoining the riverbed. The companies say they will take care of the environment, but those of us who love the river are worried. We are more than worried, we're scared shitless.

Downstream, near Ovando, a fisherperson will find trout. Fishing the Big Blackfoot has been tricky for at least the thirty years I've lived in proximity to it, but now it is stingy and erratic for even the most skilled old-timers. The Department of Fish, Wildlife, and Parks has often stocked the river, and in the riffle near our swimming hole I have caught eight-inch hatchery rainbows with notched fins. Recently, catch-and-release regulations have been instituted and seem to be successful in helping regeneration in some of the popular stretches along the Blackfoot corridor, but to hook a big native cutthroat trout is still a rare and lucky feat.

A fisheries expert told me the Big Blackfoot has the best large-river bull trout population in the nation. But that is not saying much, because bull trout are more threatened than the river. So far they have not made the endangered list, and the Endangered Species Act itself is in danger of extinction. But state, federal, and private agencies such as Trout Unlimited are doing what they can, trying to restore spawning beds choked with sediment and to help ranchers repair overgrazed tributaries and ditches that cattle have stripped of brush. Without shade to cool running water, streams run warm. Native trout cannot live in warm water.

Bull trout are an indicator species. If they go, the western-slope cutts will soon follow, and the rainbows, the owls, the elk, bear, and cougar. You can go to the Department of State Lands and see satellite photographs of the region. What you will see is a land denuded. Yet the pillage continues, most of the profits going to out-of-state corporations for short-term profits. It seems we never learn. We are determined to repeat the old boom-and-bust story of the West until nothing is left.

We need more than a plan to save the Blackfoot bioregion. We need immediate action. There is an association on the job called the Blackfoot Challenge. Its mission is "to enhance, conserve and protect the natural resources and rural lifestyle of the Blackfoot River Valley for present and future generations." Along with a steering committee headed by chairman Jim Stone of the Rolling Stone Ranch and Land Lindbergh, the Challenge works cooperatively with ranchers, state and federal natural resource managers and technicians, environmental groups, biologists, and small landholders like me.

The Blackfoot Challenge has hosted informational field trips about weed control and riparian management. It brought Senator Baucus to Dick Creek for a day of work. He helped install off-stream watering holes for livestock, skidded logs into the stream to provide overhead cover for fish, and planted willow shoots to stabilize the creek's banks.

The Challenge has initiated public meetings at community centers and rural schools in Potomac, Ovando, Helmville, Lincoln, and Seeley Lake. At the first Potomac meeting, I joined with my logger, rancher, and commuter neighbors to discuss concerns about preserving rural ways of life and work in the face of development, recreation, and conservation. If local residents who are snake-bit by *any* threat of government interference in their lives or livelihoods can be convinced that the Blackfoot Challenge will speak and work for them rather than against them, it might become a model for regional self-help.

ɔ ɔ ɔ

Recreation may not be as poisonous as cyanide, but it poses a serious danger to the river. In Norman Maclean's youth an occasional canoeist might have driven his Model T up a gravel road through the narrow, twisting slit of the Big Blackfoot's canyon to shoot Thibodeau Rapids. He would have enjoyed his day in wild solitude. This July, while the water is high enough for floating, a horde of sweaty tourists will spend half an hour to drive the same route up newly enlarged Highway 200. They will parade down the Blackfoot in Day-Glo orange rubber rafts, drink beer and pop from floating coolers, and trail strings of children in inner tubes. In his last years Maclean would not fish the lower Blackfoot because people he called "Moorish invaders from California" had desecrated his sacred places.

I too have felt outraged at strangers tramping on what seems a private preserve. But I am not on firm moral ground. I have rafted the river with my own cooler and kids in inner tubes. We shoot the rapids for the fun of it.

Speaking of shooting, sometimes I am witness to events in the Blackfoot Valley that make me wonder if everyone's gone pure loco, even the elk. Elk close up are larger than horses; their long necks and tawny colors remind me of camels. In prehistoric times elk roamed the prairies, but in our times they have survived by hiding from predatory humans in remote mountain ranges. The herd of elk that lives in the logged-over hills around my place has reverted to the instinctual pull of prairie grass, perhaps because their highland cover is gone. They come down to graze on the Potomac Valley's hay meadows when they should be in the high country: *lowland elk,* a rancher friend calls them.

Several years ago, on the opening morning of hunting

season, about fifty lowland elk grazed in a stubble field just off Highway 200. One jeepload of hunters screeched to a halt. Soon there were cars and pickups lined up the road. Guns exploded from every fence corner. A rancher in his barn ran for his rifle and joined in the blood-lust slaughter of more than thirty elk. Luckily, no person died in the crossfire. During the following weeks, local people would stumble across the decaying carcasses of eleven more elk that had been wounded, got away, but did not survive. The coyotes rejoiced; so did the vultures. The rest of us grieved.

When old ways of living on the land are abandoned, along with ancient rules of hunting and responsibility to natural life, we must invent new ways appropriate to our new values and technologies. If the river is important, so is the wild country that it runs through and so are the people who live off the country. Families who have inhabited the Blackfoot valleys for generations are puzzled. "You can barely make a living raising cattle anymore, or farming," one neighbor says. "The only thing worth a nickel is real estate."

For over a century the economy along the Blackfoot has depended on its trees: logging, mill work, driving log trucks, packaging log homes, making posts and poles. Several of my sawyer neighbors were employed by Anaconda and Champion until company crews were disbanded. These days they work as gyppo outfits and are paid by the piece. They receive no health benefits, no security, and have little economic motive to care for the land, because they know it has been logged beyond sustainability in their lifetimes. There is no place for such men in the new economy of tourism, golf courses, and condos.

Last winter I wandered into Charlie's, a favorite bar

on Higgins Avenue in Missoula. The saloon was full of young people garbed in Synchilla and decrying development. "Isn't it terrible, the way they've widened the Blackfoot Highway so RVs can get over it?" said one activist.

"I'm glad they've improved that road," I said. I drive Highway 200 almost every day and have known too many valley kids who lost their lives on the dangerous old curves at Rainbow Bend. The activist's Pavlovian response against development was no more exalted than the anti-environmental dogma of "Wise Use" junkies. Polarized attitudes have put people who share basic values at each others' throats. It's crazy.

Every year forest cover for wild animals decreases. Erosion increases. Silt chokes creeks and settles in the river. More and more folks log their woodlots and consider subdividing their land because they are out of work and need the income. Every year you can witness the transformation of country to suburb, of wild woods to industrial ugliness. I wonder if we are making a wasteland, if Norman's book and the work of historians, artists, photographers, and journalists will be the only ways our inheritors will come to know the natural diversity and beauty of this land. I wonder if humans can survive the spiritual blight of a world stripped of wild animals, trees, and pure running water.

◧ ◧ ◧

To avoid complicity in destroying what we love, we must learn all over again to adhere to the rules of right conduct. Take the day actor William Hurt came to Montana to fish the Big Blackfoot with Norman Maclean. This was in

1983, when Hurt wanted to make a film based on *A River Runs Through It*. He is a fine fly fisherman and had been preparing for the ultimate test of his fitness—playing Norman's fisherman brother, Paul, in the movie.

Bill Kittredge and I and Hurt's publicist and partner, Lois Smith, drove Hurt up the Blackfoot to Sperry Grade and, after a good bit of verbal fencing, finally got him into a rubber raft and floating downriver with Norman and his old fishing crony George Cronenbergs. Stopping on the highway so Lois could take some publicity photos, we saw the three men in a raft veer abruptly toward shore. Hurt came racing up the steep bank.

"Forgot to buy a license," he huffed.

"No fishing without a license," Norman had ruled. No matter who you are.

The run of river Hurt traversed with the two old men is protected by The Nature Conservancy. Other stretches are being conserved through easements or purchase by state, federal, and private environmental groups. Much of the Blackfoot has been designated a Wild and Scenic Rivers area, but rules and regulations, even if followed, are not enough.

Pilgrims are needed to save the sacred. Once, as part of our plan to make a film based on *A River Runs Through It,* Bill and I took producer Michael Hausman and director Richard Pearce on a location-scouting expedition with Norman. We came to where the Clearwater River flows into the Big Blackfoot and were snapping photos of a great rock, the clear water swirling around it. We were picturing Paul shadow-casting.

A young couple came striding up the bank, wicker creels over their shoulders, rods in hand. In the woman's fishing vest was a familiar paperback. "What's that book?" Mike asked.

The young couple were high school teachers from Colorado. They were retracing the fishing spots in Norman's story.

"Would you like to meet the author?" asked Mike.

Some pilgrims are not so literate. One July evening I decided to try my hand with the new fly rod my fisherman son, Eric, gave me for my birthday. Bill and I headed for the fishing spot where Norman had described his last expedition with Paul. Bill had fished that water with his own brother, and it was the salmon-fly hole where my young family had picnicked nearly twenty years before.

We walked through the woods toward a sandbar. Long-stemmed daisies and yellow buttercups glowed in the leafy light. At the head of the hole a young man stood with his left arm around a woman. His right arm moved rhythmically forward and back as he cast a line into the river. Both figures were buck naked.

I wanted to stand in the shadows and watch, wanted to see if a red coffee can full of worms lay at the man's feet like the one Jessie's naked, drunk, and sunburnt brother Neal used in *A River Runs Through It*. Bill pulled me away.

The sweet acrid odor of decaying cottonwood leaves reminded me of days when I walked the Blackfoot with David Smith and Dick Hugo and Norman Maclean—all of them gone. Bill stooped to pick up a soggy wallet with a driver's license and a man's picture dated three years before. We had visions of death on the river, and love, at the same moment.

Connecting with a river means learning to float. You think you know where you're going, and then you encounter an unexpected turn, a current or flood; you are swept under; you emerge transformed by the act of surviving danger. The river hides rocks and deep snags and drowned creatures, and it is this secrecy that draws me— the tension between what's on the surface and what lies beneath. I believe we are more like rivers than we are like meadows.

Floating on my back down the Blackfoot on a dog day in August, I like to point my toes downstream and look up to cliffs and clouds. A red-tailed hawk sails above me. I float past silver-plumed willows. Blue dragonflies hover above a riffle. A kingfisher with his crested, outsized head dives for a minnow. Immersed in liquid light I find relief from self and time.

Each of us has memories we sing over and over again like a song in our inner ear. If your place of memory and connection is the Big Blackfoot River you are blessed, as I am. You will want to do what you can to save the river so your grandchildren can float its green waters and fish its native cutthroats and bull trout. You will teach them to dive into deep pools, touch stones that go back to the beginnings of time. The river is not dead yet. Boys and girls should make love on its banks.

The Rites of Snow

Who can explain the euphoria of snow-lovers? Our black lab puppy Shy Moon came new with us to our Montana homestead in the winter of 1970, and she'd leap and roll and burrow into snowbanks like a wag-tailed otter. Shy Moon's run of mongrels—Bagel, Mocha, Goatee—and the two shepherd dogs who live with me now, Rasta and Betty Boop, are no different. Snow falls and they dance into it. They open their mouths to catch snowflakes on their tongues, chase snowballs, dive into drifts and come up white-nosed, hoary, tingling. The dogs are laughing, like me. Like my sons.

The boys come home for Christmas if they can. All four are grown now and living in Maryland, Austin, Iowa City, Kalispell. I never go out on a Christmas tree hunt until the twins, Alex and Andrew, arrive. It's a ritual that began twenty-three years ago when they were four years old, our first winter on the ranch. We headed into the woods on snowshoes through four-foot drifts. Dave was short of breath from the heart disease, but he led the way, an ax slung over his shoulder. Eric and Steve, gangling, long-haired, and hip at fifteen and thirteen, pulled the little ones on our new toboggan, a gift from their grandparents.

Every winter we search for the perfect, full-limbed fir

or pine that must touch the log beams of our living room. We do not worry about conserving young trees, for they are abundant in our forest, third growth. It's the old ones we prize and protect, the few ancient survivors of a century of logging. These winters my sons are nearly as tall as the trees they chop down, and they carry the fragrant, snow-damp load a quarter mile up the logging road to home.

The ritual continues with bluegrass on the tape deck, the trimming of boughs, stringing of lights (my job), and a life's accumulation of ornaments to hang. Each ornament has a history. There's a painted Santa nearly fifty years old from my childhood in Chicago; enameled tin fruit—purple grapes, red cherries, yellow bananas—from a trip to Oaxaca; handmade yarn bells from the country school my boys attended in the hamlet of Potomac; Hmong hangings from Missoula fairs; a ceramic Flathead angel; imitation birds; clusters of miniature felt oranges.

As I stand precariously on a stepladder to hang a candy cane, I remember decorating a tree in Seattle when I was as young as the twins are now, already a mother of two and dead broke. David was in graduate school and we lived on Magnolia Bluff in a tilting house overlooking Puget Sound. I gathered white shells from our beach, and bits of blue and amber sea-rounded glass, and fastened them to the tree with wire. I strung red holly berries stolen from a neighbor's bushes with popcorn to garland the tree. We lit it with birthday candles bedded safely in aluminum foil. Two-year old Steve in his red pajamas was so flushed with the excitement of his new tricycle that we didn't real-ize until late in the afternoon that he'd run up a fever of nearly 104 degrees.

Christmas fever can turn dangerous on you any time,

which is what the white-haired woman hanging her candy canes knows only too well.

᎘   ᎘   ᎘

Snow ended the dog days of August this year, two inches on my deck, the violet and fuchsia petunias fringed with white; white frosting on the strawberries and squash blossoms, and in the evergreen hills young firs and ponderosas drooped like weeping willows with their burdens of untimely snow. It is called the August singularity—a sudden cold front from Canada that signals the end of summer.

On August 21 my meadow was baked brown; the pine hills that circle our homestead were crackling dry from a month of blue-sky days in the nineties. On August 22 the temperature dropped into the thirties, snow fell, and that night we began the rites of winter. Andrew, my niece Celia, and a few young visitors clustered around the brick fireplace. Gin gave way to Jim Beam, white wine to red. We wrapped ourselves in afghans, dug sweaters out of mothballs, and threw logs on the fire. I shed the torpor of summer like a snake sheds her skin and rejoiced in the buzz of energy, the excitement that comes with first snow in any season.

Living at 4,000 feet in the foothills of the northern Rockies, I've seen snow on the Fourth of July, snow in September, but only this once in August. Perhaps it's a sign from the weather gods, for snow has become a dwindling commodity. We've suffered a ten-year drought, open winters, the boring grey sky over mud and leafless trees. Mountain snowpacks are down, stream flows are lower than ever, forests burn, and ranchers battle fishermen for what water remains. Maybe it's the dreaded greenhouse effect, maybe El Niño currents, maybe the snow will come back—the sweet snows of yesteryear.

Twenty-four years ago we shoveled paths through waist-high drifts to feed chickens or to reach the outhouse. We were building the big house and lived in a one-room log bunkhouse with a loft: four boys, two dogs, two cats, and hippie parents. We melted snow for water, cooked on a Coleman gas stove, and could not see over the snow-fat road banks thrown high as a car by the snowplow. In February the county quit plowing our drive, and the Land Rover was stuck in the middle of the road for a month. We snowshoed half a mile from the end of the county road to our cabin, carrying coal and groceries in backpacks.

Friends in town pitied us, but Dave and I were happy with our chosen burden. The work of day-to-day living in backcountry winter turned our energies outward. Cutting wood, feeding stock, keeping vehicles running—these were physical chores that bound the family into a unit. The mental beasts of fear—fear of fatal illness, fear of fracture and separation—had to linger in the cold starlight beyond the fires we built to keep ourselves warm.

Life is easier these days, and I have exchanged the necessity of snowshoes for the sport of skis. I learned to cross-country ski in deep snow and taught my kids to follow in my tracks. When they come home for Christmas the yard is thick with skis and poles. We've been lucky, because even in these dry years, what snow has come has fallen in December.

Our meadow is a natural bowl sloping down from wooded cliffs. I get into shape by cutting trails up the meadow and through the trees. I've wrecked my right knee

by schussing down an icy track into a barbed wire fence.
Years earlier I tore the ligaments in both knees by trying to
brake a runaway toboggan loaded with little boys by sticking my feet into the hard-crusted snow. It was a tough
lesson in the art of sliding. Limp for two months and you
will learn to go with the terrain, turn into it, but not
force a stop.

After a Christmas morning of opening presents in
front of the fire, drinking mimosas, munching on croissants
and the bittersweet chocolate-dipped orange peels that are
my holiday specialty, we head for the skis. If we are lucky,
the meadow is sparkling in the sun, hoarfrost gilding tall
grass and the wild hawthorne. We are blessed with a field
of snow out every door. The two-story log house with its
steeply pitched shake roof stands like an ocean liner in its
rolling white sea.

Bill usually stays by the fire. He learned to ski in Oregon but has given up snow sport for the green precision of
golf (too many years spent feeding cows in a blizzard) and
prefers to sit in his armchair browsing the new Christmas
books. The standing roast of prime rib he has brought is
in the oven. Old friends will arrive soon to join our traditional feast of rare beef and Yorkshire pudding, whipped
cream with horseradish, red cranberries, green broccoli,
fresh baked bread, and at least two kinds of pie made by
the boys—apple and pecan, or pumpkin, sometimes
mincemeat.

ɕ   ɕ   ɕ

Our first great feast on the ranch was Thanksgiving of
1971. There was not enough room in the cabin for all of us

and our out-of-town guests, along with our carpenter/
writer friends who were helping us build the big house.
We'd been making doors and windows in a cavernous
cement-block garage built to house the former owner's logging rig and stock truck. It was just barely heated by two
woodstoves, but we set up trestle tables, borrowed a second
Coleman stove, and cooked.

The menu centered on wild foods hunted, fished,
and gathered in our new abode: trout from the Blackfoot
River, grouse from the woods, meadow mushrooms and
shaggymanes. I improvised a juniper berry sauce for the
game and baked apple pies with the fruit of the tree gone
wild on our meadow. We sweetened our bread with fresh
huckleberry preserves. We ate in mittens and wool caps.
We gave thanks as the first blizzard of the year covered
our small world with six inches of white.

We moved into the new house on Christmas day the
next year. It wasn't finished. A wool blanket covered the
door to the living room, where we had spread our mattresses on floorboards salvaged from the Hellgate High
School gym. The worn maple was marked with random
green and yellow stripes, red numbers, like a Mondrian
painting. We rejoiced in the perfume of red cedar from our
new shake roof, also electric heat.

The kitchen wing had no glass in the windows, and
plastic sheathing gave scant protection from winter winds.
The plumbing had not yet been connected, and I cooked
our pot roast on a Coleman gas stove. Still, we celebrated.
The tree stood gaily in the corner, lights blinking, and the
table was spread with goodies. I missed the intimate
warmth of our one-room cabin, but this new house would
be beautiful, spacious, solid as rock.

That was the last Christmas we would share together in our new house. The following winter, Dave, Steve, the twins, and I were in Hollywood. We had rented a one-bedroom furnished apartment in a transients' building on Orchid Street, leaving Eric to finish high school and oversee the young renters on our ranch. Dave had quit his tenured position at the university, and we were embarked on a last desperate try to make daydreams come true. Dave knew he did not have much time. He was determined to break into the movies, which we could not do long-distance.

"It's Disneyland," said Dave. "We can always go back to Montana." He wrote scripts and I looked for film work and Steve endured Hollywood High. By April Fool's Day, we had come back to Montana, broke, stripped of illusions, and wondering what our next move should be. Dave never got a chance to decide.

    ❏   ❏   ❏

Only one Smith is religious in any conventional sense. Stephen is a devout Catholic, revived through the church from troubles too deep to bear without faith. He goes to midnight mass in Missoula, and sometimes the twins and I go with him. It's a beautiful way to praise rebirth and salvation, the families gathered in their finest, incense and candles burning, a choir singing like angels. My parents, Jewish by birth and in culture, never practiced the religion except to honor their Old Country parents. David was a failed Baptist, and the rest of us worship God or whatever we call sacred in our private and personal ways.

To thank the old year and welcome the new, we throw a great party during the week between Christmas and New

Year's. We invite old friends and new ones, graduate students who aspire to be writers, faculty from the University of Montana, where Dave taught and where Bill still teaches. There are old folks and teenagers, young adults with toddlers, those of us in middle age. Someone always brings strangers from Japan or France, England, Australia, Hollywood.

I prepare vats of chili made with pinto beans. When Steve was home we'd have venison in the pot, for he is the large-game hunter in the family. Other times we make do with short ribs of beef and ground meat. The rest is pot luck: cornbread, salads of every variety, chips and dips, veggies, and pies. I'll buy a keg of beer and gallon jugs of wine. Sometimes there's rum for hot drinks, always hot cider for kids and teetotalers. Coffee and cocoa send folks home somewhat sober and belly-warmed.

Before we get down to chow, we must earn our hunger with winter sports. As the sun dips over a western ridge, partygoers take to the meadow and logging roads on skis. Children slide down the gentle slopes in sleds, black rubber innertubes, snowboards. One year when the snow barely covered rocks and grass so we couldn't ski, the boys set up their net, and we had a raucous game of snow volleyball, people sliding, leaping, collapsing in laughter in the freezing dusk.

Serious tobogganing happens only after dark. Our twenty-year-old sled is missing boards, and it's time for Santa Claus to grace the family with a new toboggan. Often the twins, Eric and his wife Becca, and Steve have prepared a track in advance. On a good snow year the run will begin on the upper meadow near the stone pile, jump the road, and continue on a steep pitch until the course levels out at the barbed wire fence that arbitrarily splits our ground from the neighbor's.

The two places were one a century ago, when the Swedish immigrants who homesteaded our land celebrated their first Christmas. The fires they built were the only lights in a forest full of wild animals that circled for miles and miles. Christ Tandborg and Anders Anderson and their families cleared a rectangle in the virgin woods to make hay meadows and grain fields and began the endless task of picking rocks from the clay soil that runs one hundred feet deep. Left to itself the meadow is beginning its return to forest, but the work of human hands calls out for respect, so I have made a bargain with ghosts. We'll allow patches of brush and young pines to form islands of cover for bluebirds, coyotes, chipmunks, and the rabbits and mice whose trails cross ours in the snow. The pine, fir, and larch forest will remain untouched except as a place to collect firewood and Christmas trees. Elk, white-tails and mule deer, black bears, and the occasional moose or mountain lion will find those woods a refuge from hunters and loggers. But we will continue to clear the meadow, graze summer cattle and our two old mares on it, harvest our twenty fenced acres of hay, and cling to a tradition that values nurture over greed.

Such clinging isn't easy when alien seeds are germinating under the pristine white. Knapweed, leafy spurge, Russian thistle, and a sulphur-yellow cinquefoil have been brought in on the wheels of logging trucks that cross my land winter and summer. You might think it's a pretty sight—acres of lavender knapweed, acres of yellow petals— but the roots of these plants poison grass. They have no natural enemies, for they too are immigrants, carried into

the West stuck on shoe soles or burlap sacks with cargo
from Yugoslavia, Iran, the Siberian steppes.

As I ski among the seed heads I decide to do what I
have never done. When the weeds bolt in July, I'm going to
attack them with herbicide. No one, not even a determined
environmentalist gentlewoman homesteader, wants to see
her land go sterile.

ट ट ट

One evening a couple of years ago during our holiday
party, when the meadow was laced with lavender shadows
from the setting sun, I skied with a friend across the rose-
tinted snowfields. We could hear the whoops of young
tobogganers preparing for the night's sport. My two shepherd dogs and my friend Bob's bird dog followed in our
tracks. My friend is a professor of linguistics.

"Annick," he called from the top of the ridge, "it's
worth three thousand dollars."

"What's worth three thousand dollars?"

"This," he said, pointing his pole toward the setting
sun and sweeping it forward to encompass the meadow,
the woods, the high peaks of the Bob Marshall Wilderness
on the eastern horizon.

"One run on this place—this view, these friends—it's
worth the three thousand more I'd be making at any other
university."

My friend was being modest; the difference would
be ten thousand dollars, for the pleasures of snow carry
a high price. Montana has always been a natural resource
colony for coupon-clippers in New York, Chicago, Los
Angeles, Tokyo, Berlin. They take our timber, our coal,

our copper, our gold, our water. They hunt elk, fish for native trout, overrun our wilderness. We are left with boom-and-bust work in the woods and mines, servant jobs like making beds for tourists—bottom-dollar for professionals. There is no prosperous future for most of our children.

What remains is the joy. We walk in space—a state six hundred miles across with fewer than 850,000 inhabitants. People recognize us on the streets. When we call our one congressman, our senators, our governor, they know our names. Our children want to come home, like the Native Americans who are returning to reservations to make a better life in the place that has always been theirs and sacred.

Those who take the chance may not be able to buy land if they're coming home to the Flathead, the Bitterroot, the Clark Fork, the Blackfoot, or the Gallatin valleys. Retirees from overpopulated and polluted shores and celebrities seeking hideaways from the neon world, have driven real estate so high that locals can't afford the taxes. Can't afford to move. We writers and artists who have let the cat out of the bag are complicit. So we try to discourage would-be immigrants by talking about winter.

"You don't understand what winter means," we say, hoping the newcomers will carry their baggage to the Sun Belt. "It snows in August. It snows on the Fourth of July."

When summer ends and the tourists ride off in their motor homes and the highways are slick with black ice, hard-core Montanans begin our six-month winter dances. Bars fill up with blue-lipped men and women in parkas and boots. We drink too much, eat red meat, smoke any weed. We collect unemployment and spend hours jump-starting stalled rigs. We swear we'll move to Arizona. We pray for snow.

It is this mix of festivity and danger, sparkle and dread that draws me so close to winter, to mountains, to Montana. When you can see your breath, you know you are alive.

Country and Western

Almost everything has changed on Missoula's Front Street.
The grand Art Deco Florence Hotel is now the Glacier
General Building, home office of lawyers and insurance
adjusters. Across the way, where Missoula's long-gone
riverfront cathouses once thronged with cowboys, loggers,
and railroaders, college kids and upscale wives sip double
cappuccinos. And where Luke's biker bar once hosted
bluegrass sing-alongs, forty-five-year-old anachronisms
from the sixties, their long greasy hair turned gray, pan-
handle from old ladies who live in the high-rise senior
citizens' home.

But we are not going to get nostalgic or depressed this
clear-skied October evening. It's Friday night in Missoula.
High school kids are cruising the drag up and down Higgins Avenue. The streets are crowded with Homecoming
locals celebrating a Montana Grizzlies football victory. Bill
and I have put on our dancing shoes. The Mudflaps are
swinging at the refurbished Top Hat Lounge, and it's
going to be hot times in the old town tonight.

The first time I saw the Mudflaps perform was nearly
twenty years ago when the old Top Hat was as unregener-
ate as me and my hard-drinking, pot-smoking pals. This
dance-hall saloon was as close as Missoula could imagine to
Chicago's Aragon Ballroom, where Dave and I once cut a

rug under a velvet canopy dotted with electric stars to the swing beat of Tommy Dorsey's band.

The bad old Top Hat did not have velvet or stars, it had frescoes. Jay Rummel, a ceramist and visual artist whose provincial fame goes back to the high days of the sixties, had painted its walls with elongated cartoons of local dropouts and druggies disguised as western outlaws. Now the frescoes have been covered with grooved knotty pine, but they are alive in my memory, vivid as the night I went dancing alone.

"There's a new group from the Bitterroot," some young friends of musical persuasion had informed me. "You'll be sorry if you miss this one. And don't wear your eight-pound hiking boots."

"Sure," I said. "Are you kidding? A great new group from Hamilton, Montana?" But I was bored after a year of widow's mourning, ready to cut loose with no lover or date or ties to bind me. And on the long narrow strip of polished dance floor in front of the raised bandstand, surrounded by flaking plaster inscribed with Rummel's mountain men and shady ladies, I wore out a new pair of wool socks. I jitterbugged, foxtrotted, and drunkenly improvised to the ebullient, funky swing of this happy new discovery from the Bitterroot Valley.

Big Sky Mudflaps. The name conjures images of loggers in thick-soled work boots, or truck drivers in tandem twenty-two-wheel semis scattering stockyard odors down the interstate. Or country families in mud-splattered pickups cruising backhills dirt roads for firewood, deer, or wild huckleberries. It does not bring to mind David Horgan in a Hawaiian shirt, strumming an electric guitar; or slim Beth Lo in a polka-dot forties dress, beating accompaniment on a bass fiddle; or Maureen Powell, be-bopping "Flippity Flop Flop" on her bass guitar. Where did they come from, I wondered, this mellow swing-jazz band with the funky clothes and old-time tunes like "Lady Be Good" and "Sentimental Gentleman from Georgia"?

It seems the Mudflaps were friends and friends of friends who emigrated to Hamilton about the same time Dave and I came to Missoula. In the mid-sixties the idyllic Bitterroot Valley was still agricultural ranchlands, one of Montana's best-kept promises. The valley was a hideout for radicals of all persuasions: headquarters for the John Birch Society, a haven for polygamous Mormons, a place for Utopian hippie communes. This was before the chic Hollywood contingent arrived. Before nest-egg retirees and California refugees had divided the green, mountain-fringed meadows into country estates, one-acre ranchettes, and trailer parks.

Word got around about the new band, as it does in these parts, for there are very few secrets in western Montana when it comes to anyone's favorite watering hole or musical group. Soon the Flaps were making the forty-five-mile trip to Missoula every weekend, playing the Top Hat and the old Park Hotel, and everyone was dancing.

As the Mudflaps got more popular, they became more ambitious, but never so serious they would give up actual lives for full-time on-the-road entertainment. Beth Lo and her husband Dave Horgan have become my friends. Beth is a ceramic artist who teaches at the University of Montana; Dave is a writer. Like me, they chose community over ambition—a familiar pattern in a place where scenery counts for wages. That's why so many of us graying flower children are still here, still surviving on marginal incomes, still content with our fates.

One of the good things about music these hi-tech electronic days is that tracks can be recorded anywhere. All you need is a state-of-the-art sound studio and technicians who know what they're doing. Regional recording can be as accessible as regional publishing, and also as financially erratic. The Mudflaps recorded their first album, *Armchair Cabaret,* at Bitterroot Recording in Missoula, an outfit that made records for the Mission Mountain Wood Band, country singer Jan Del, and even my neighbor Terry Rae, who lives a mile or so down Bear Creek.

So, if you don't live in Montana where the Mudflaps hang out when they're not on the road, or if you do and it's ten below zero, the roads are black ice, you have a friend staying over and a good fire in the wood-burning stove, you don't have to get out of the house to boogie. You can lean back in your armchair, as I recline in mine, and smooth out to old favorites like "Is You Is or Is You Ain't My Baby?" or original tunes in the old mold, like Dave Horgan's "Admiral Byrd's Blues." You might be in the Big Apple or sitting at the bottom of the world. Wherever you are, if you like to tap your toes or take a trip to Montana's bad old swinging days, you are bound to like the Mudflaps.

⸎   ⸎   ⸎

Recorded tunes are fine in winter, but when sun finally melts Mount Sentinel's snows, there is no substitute for live music in the Big Sky out-of-doors. Fresh-air concerts have been standard in western Montana as long as I can remember. There are oom-pah-pah marches from the bandstand in Bonner Park, where families picnic; Indian powwows at Fort Missoula with wailing Blackfeet drummers and Salish and Kootenai fancy dancers; country singers and rednecks at the Mule Palace near Arlee; and a pricey festival in Whitefish for tourists and upscale locals that imports such stars as Emmylou Harris and Robert Cray. But the high (and I do mean high) pitch of musical euphoria that reigned in Missoula during the seventies has never been surpassed.

Take the Blackfoot Boogie, an annual summer orgy that ended with the last gasps of hippiedom and the first bites of environmental activism to touch this region. Eric and Steve, my hip teenage sons, took me to the last concert, just past Whittaker Bridge, a mile or so downstream and across the river from the fishing hole by Belmont Creek that was sacred to Norman Maclean and the Smith family, also.

It was my second widow summer. In youth I never had a chance to be wild like other girls I knew. When I met Dave at Jane Addams's Hull House, I was sixteen, a high school volunteer doing a sociology project. Dave, at nineteen, was working his way through the University of Chicago by teaching Puerto Rican boys the fine points of basketball. We fell into love and lust, went steady, got married three years later. At twenty-two, I had given birth to two children, which cramps a girl's style.

Although young motherhood has become a class marker in the 1990s, reserved for unwed teenage girls who are usually poor and often "of color," it was common for middle-class gals in the 1950s. So at thirty-nine, although I had tasted illicit romance and harbored secret longings, I felt I had missed my opportunity for profligate flaming youth. Which may explain why I put aside my widow grief and decided to initiate myself into the rituals of being single, white, and liberated.

The concert scene was a meadow on a cliff above the Blackfoot River. It swarmed with sweaty celebrants, some mellow from hash, pot, and beer, some jumping with hard booze and speed. "Here, have a hit of this Columbia Gold," said a man I had seen around town for years but never actually talked to. He offered me his pipe. The man wore shorts, and his graying ponytail grazed his tie-dyed T-shirt.

I had several hits and in a state of heightened aware-ness inhaled the smells of reefer and river, trampled grass and spilled beer. I remember being mesmerized by glowing particles of dust. I danced with younger men and clapped my hands to the rousing bluegrass of the Mission Mountain Wood Band. Eric would soon become a roadie for that band, and he introduced me to the players, most of whom would die in a plane crash one ill-fated Fourth of July. Steve Riddle, the lead singer, had been in the junior English class I had taught at Sentinel High School in 1967—posi-tively my worst student, always stoned, insolent, and rebellious. Now he played a song for me, "In Without Knocking," inspired by a painting by Charlie Russell in which a mounted cowpoke crashes into a Wild West bar lit yellow in the night.

A coterie of whacked-out naked couples made a great show of jumping off cliffs into the river. I was offended by their smugness, the cheap thrills of flaunting convention. I knew valley neighbors whose sons had drowned in just such a drunken display. I understood sorrow. But I was most offended by revelers who tossed Styrofoam cups and aluminum cans into clumps of wildflowers—violets and forget-me-nots, and the scarlet Indian paintbrush I loved to pick for bouquets.

"Look at those damned Porta-Potties!" I exclaimed. The bright blue vessels of excrement were propped like upright coffins along my sacred river.

"Oh, Mom!"

I don't know if Eric and Steve were pleased to see me react in such a predictable Mom way, or merely dismayed. My glow had worn off. "Party's over," I said.

I turned my leased Chevy Blazer into a stream of off-road vehicles that bumped through the woods along the rutted gravel road bordering the Blackfoot. There was no fun for me in desecrating a place I loved. I was glad to get home before dark.

"No," I told my boys later, when their buddies urged them to host a bluegrass concert kegger on our meadow. Just say no to the spoiling of Eden.

ɔ   ɔ   ɔ

Country bars are more to my liking. The Awful Burger Bar in Potomac was our local watering trough, until it was torn down and rebuilt as an A-frame gas station, quick-stop store, restaurant and bar. It sits just off Highway 200 on a jack-pine flat facing south across irrigated hay meadows to where what's left of the town of Potomac clusters around the red brick elementary school. The owners blew up the original log bungalow with dynamite as an exercise for rural firefighters.

I remember a Fourth of July at the Awful Burger when Dave was still alive. All the regulars were there, and families from the valley. Kids ran in and out as they do in Montana, where a country bar serves as the local community center. Firecrackers exploded in the gravel parking lot, and college students from Missoula danced cowboy boogie. It was nine at night, but the sun streamed in through open doors and windows. One of the young men in the band began to juggle lemons in time to the music—"Mommas Don't Let Your Babies Grow Up to Be Cowboys."

Many of my best friends, especially male writers over fifty, feel most at home in western bars. "Home. Home, I knew it entering," is the opening line of Dick Hugo's poem, "The Only Bar in Dixon." It was no accident Hugo rented his first Montana dwelling in a shabby loggers' compound next door to Harold's Milltown Bar, Laundromat, and Cafe.

When Dave and I, Eric and Steve, arrived in Missoula in 1964, we landed on Hugo's doorstep and slept on air mattresses strung along the linoleum floor of his apartment. We parked our VW bus in the bar's lot. The rig was loaded to the roof with boxes of books, and loud with the barking of our German shepherd, Sylvie, and her ten eight-week-old pups.

Dick initiated us into the country delights of the Milltown Bar, and we drank Beam ditches (bourbon and water), played songs about whiskey, work, and lost women on the jukebox, and heard a millworker's story about a hunting trip turned nightmare when a lame grizzly known as "Three Toes" ate his companion. The only retrievable parts of our storyteller's hunting pal were the indigestible metal snaps off his boxer shorts.

Hugo's poem, "The Milltown Union Bar (Laundromat and Cafe)," says:

Country and Western

You need never leave. Money or a story
brings you booze. The elk is grinning
and the goat says go so tenderly
you hear him through the glass. If you weep
deer heads weep. Sing and the orphanage
announces plans for your release. A train
goes by and ditches jump. You were nothing
going in and now you kiss your hand.

Although Dick is drinking in heaven, the poem he
wrote still hangs, dog-eared and sheathed in plastic, above
the cash register.

◧   ◧   ◧

In Montana, country and western songs became my second
language. Most, it seemed, were written just for me. A few
years after Dave died, Bill Kittredge and I courted each
other with Merle Haggard singing "All My Friends Are
Going to Be Strangers" on the radio. We drank and danced
at the AmVets and the Cabin, took the twins to hear our
favorite singers—Willie Nelson, Doc Watson, Jerry Jeff
Walker—at university concerts.

When Ernest Tubb came to town on his final tour,
of course we went. The bar was Turah Pines, a few miles
down the dirt road from Milltown. It is pure country,
walled in yellow-varnished knotty pine, hung with deer
heads, etched with local brands. Tubb's backup band wore
red satin cowboy shirts with white arrows stitched on
the pockets. Both the shirts and the band members had
seen better days. The lead guitarist was almost bald. The
bass man wore a corset. The second guitar was young

and long-legged, with acne on his face—maybe Ernest's
son. But the fat man playing pedal steel could still break
your heart.

When the band struck up "Waltz Across Texas"
early in the night, Bill and I waltzed through to the end.
Later we watched an older couple dressed in matching
jeans and pressed shirts. The man's hair was slicked
back; the woman's bottle-yellow hair blossomed in a
halo of permed curls. They twirled and dipped in perfect sync. You could tell they were fine-tuned, practiced
as a team of circus ponies. We sat out the fast dances
but got up on our feet with the rest of the crowd
when Ernest Tubb sang "I'm Walking the Floor over
You."

He closed the show with "Rainbow at Midnight." I
had never heard the song before, and it stuck in my mind
as some songs will:

After the war was over,
I was coming home to you.
I saw a rainbow at midnight,
Out on the ocean blue.

The words were sentimental, and I wondered what in
hell a rainbow at midnight could be. But the ending
touched me:

After this life is over
And our journey here is through,
We'll move to the land of the rainbow
And live in the starry blue.

To live in the starry blue, I thought, is what we all
desire. I found myself weeping. "It's not your fault," I said,
laughing at the confounded way Bill was looking at me.

◧   ◧   ◧

Years later I saw an actual rainbow at midnight. Bill and
I were driving back from a cultural conference in Helena
called "Montana Myths: Sacred Stories, Sacred Cows," a
conference that introduced us to Mary Clearman Blew,
Richard Roeder, Bill Lang—writers and scholars who
would become dear friends. During that moonlit drive
Bill and I decided to try to put together an anthology of
Montana literature for the state's centennial. For the next
four years we would work with Mary, Rich, and Bill, as
well as with our Missoula compatriots, Bill Bevis and Jim
Welch, in compiling and editing *The Last Best Place.*

Life is indeed a circle, or better yet, a spiral. The rain-
bow at midnight that Bill and I saw—white light arching
through a cloudburst above moonstruck hills—passed over
Rock Creek. Which is where Dave and I had lived with
Eric and Steve, where I had conceived the twins, Alex and
Andrew.

And when my eldest son, Eric, married Becca in 1989,
we swung to the music of the Big Sky Mudflaps in the living room of our log house. The kids chose to be married
on Memorial Day weekend in honor of the traditional
Memorial Day parties that Dave and I had started our
first year on the ranch, and which I continue to celebrate
most every spring. Usually there are softball games in the
meadow, a keg on the porch, potluck in the sun. But this
Memorial Day a cold rain poured down.

We and our hundred-plus guests would not be squelched. Champagne flowed. A crowd gathered around the newlyweds. We joined hands in a circle. The floors shook and our massive log walls jumped as we danced round and round until night became dawn.

In the Garden with Beasts

Elk venture out of the hills in May to graze the new grass
on my meadow. When huckleberries ripen, black bears
raid the shrubs at the borders of my homestead ranch. I can
hear coyotes howling all through the year, and on crystal
winter days with an Arctic storm blowing into Montana at
thirty degrees below zero, it is easy to think I am truly out
in the wilderness.

I'm not. From every window I look to logged-off hills.
I have electricity and telephones and neighbors. Missoula,
with an urban area approaching 70,000, is only twenty-five
miles down the highway. To find the *real* outback you must
abandon roads, carry food and shelter on your back, and
walk. The best walking is with family, friends, and lovers.
Take children and dogs; take a camera. Hike until your
breath fails and your legs seem to move with a will of their
own. Pitch your tent as dark falls. Eat cheese, spaghetti, and
chocolate. Drink brandy by an open fire. Sleep under stars.

Years ago, Dave and I spent three days hiking with
our Seattle friends the Stadlers and the Dougalls on the
wild Pacific shores of Vancouver Island. Dave was just out
of the University of Washington's hospital, weak from the
liquid diet doctors had been giving him to test cholesterol-
lowering drugs. We walked on sand turned to stone,
orange-tinged shelves along the ocean. We studied purple

starfish and the green waving tendrils of sea anemones. Dave carried a pack like the rest of us. If he had a heart attack there would be no way to get help.

"It's fine," said Dave. "I'm where I want to be."

The Pacific Northwest was my first real taste of the wild. While Dave was in graduate school, we lived in a Seattle housing project rife with poverty and crime, and the Olympic Peninsula's beaches with their sea stacks, thronging life, and native peoples were our getaway supreme. When he was six months old, Steve drank formula from a fire-blackened bottle at the edge of the Pacific. My first backpacking trip took place the next February, a twenty-two-mile wilderness beach hike from LaPush to Lake Ozette.

Dave and I bought cheap canvas Trapper Nelson packs. With the Dougalls, Anne Stadler, Dave's old college roommate Dave Nash, and a Quaker lawyer, Bill Hansen, we packed in heavy cans of spaghetti. We got lost on headlands in a jungle of salal. Next morning, while the tide was out, like idiots we drank wine and sang hymns. By afternoon a winter squall had roared in with the tide. We huddled on a rock cliff with no shelter or fire, no way to move until the tide abated. We called that trip the "Death March" and bored anyone who'd listen with gleeful stories of our misadventures.

Dave and I returned to LaPush, Lake Ozette, and the Makah Reservation again and again. While Neil Armstrong took his "one great step for mankind," the Smith and Stadler families sat on piles of driftwood at LaPush and studied the full moon. Other trips we fished for salmon, flew kites in March, gathered clams and mussels, watched gray whales. And after Dave died, the Dougalls and I repeated a more hair-raising version of the winter death march with eleven-year-old Alex and Andrew.

I still go back to those revered beaches with the boys, with Bill and his kids and grandkids. But the Northwest was just the beginning of a lifelong pattern of camp-out pilgrimages. At five, Eric caught a huge lake trout up in the British Columbia bush and became so enamored of the sport that fly-fishing has influenced his choice of jobs and where to live. When Alex and Andrew were twelve, Bill and I led them to the top of Sperry Glacier in Glacier National Park. We looked down to mountain peaks and hanging gardens. The frozen earth was blue-white and glowing all around as we ate our tuna sandwiches. And last August when Steve and I hiked into Glacier Park's low-lying Kootenai Lakes, we found ourselves neighbors with a wide-racked bull moose, a cow, and a calf. The moose family stood knee-deep in the green, swampy waters about fifty yards from our campground, slurping up bottom-weeds. All night long, Steve and I would wake in our two-person pup tent to the sounds of low, grunting moosetalk.

Now I am nearing sixty and I don't go camping as often as I would like. My boys are men and off on their own adventures. Bill, who has shared my life since 1978, would rather be golfing; and I have a bad right knee (cross-country skiing) and two wrecked ankles. But one day I hope to be a grandmother. I have plans for camping with grandkids and stories to tell them.

◘   ◘   ◘

In the summer of 1986, while the twins were home from college, I gathered our Smith tribe for an exploration into the Jewel Basin, a region of mountains and azure lakes at the western edge of the Bob Marshall Wilderness near Bigfork. It was August and over 90 degrees, and we got a late start, as usual. The twins and I threw our gear and Rasta, our three-month-old German shepherd, into the Subaru, headed north and stopped to pick up Eric and his girlfriend in Kalispell. By the time we hit the trail it was nearly five o'clock. "No problem," said Eric, our guide on this expedition. "It's just a short hike to the first fishing lake."

The sun blazed in a white sky, and the high pine woods, tinder-dry from a three-year drought, seemed to crackle. It was so hot I decided to leave my heavy hiking boots in the car and proceed in tennis shoes. My borrowed backpack was the lightest of all, but daunting enough for a middle-aged smoker. Then we discovered that instead of four miles, we were looking at maybe six. A cooking pot poked into my back as I tried to adjust my unbalanced load.

We trudged through ponderosa pines on a good trail, the pup racing from front person to tail person as if herding sheep. On the uphill grades I sweated and huffed and puffed, but then the sky darkened and a squall cooled our way—like the spray of a lawn sprinkler, lovely. We climbed into a mountain meadow where the lush grass bloomed with yellow-bells and magenta shooting stars. Red Indian paintbrush and blue lupine clustered along a meandering gravel-bedded creek. The air was sweet from rain. Dark granite peaks rose to the horizon.

The trail wound down to a mucky green lake. Not what I'd hoped for. "Is that it?"

"No fish in this one," said Eric.

So we began to climb again. I straggled behind my striding six-foot sons. Even the dog was dragging. The

showers had made the trail slippery and my bum knee
hurt. At the top I stopped for breath. The main trail kept to
the ridge skirting the mountains; a side trail zigzagged
steeply down through wild-rose thickets to a round lake
that shone sapphire blue in the setting sun, one of the many
jewel lakes that give this basin its name.

The kids were halfway to the lake when I began the
long, steep trail down. Going down can be harder than
going up; weakening limbs strain to support your weight
against the pull of gravity. Andrew waited for me while the
others went ahead to make camp. The tents were going up.
Eric had started a cooking fire. Andrew and I talked about
food—shish-kabobs for dinner, maybe rainbow trout for
breakfast.

Twenty-five yards from shore, "like a cow headed for
the barn," Eric said later, I took a shortcut through rank
wet weeds. My left foot gave way. My pack swung me like
a corkscrew around my planted right leg. I heard a snap.
My right ankle.

"Andrew!" I called. "Andrew, come here." He turned
around. "It's broke."

Andrew laughed, incredulous. "Yah, sure, it's broke."

I will disturb you with a few details—double fracture,
cracked heel, tendons torn away. We fashioned a splint
from two stout sticks and tied it with my bandana. I had
chills from the shock; swallowed aspirin and broth. Eric's
prescription anti-inflammatory drug for his sore shoulder
kept the swelling down. I drank brandy and more brandy.
The twins carried me into the brush to pee. It was a long
night.

At daybreak Eric and Andrew hiked out to find help.
Alex and I tried reading books as the sun rose; we studied

the ridge through binoculars; we watched birds and waited. At last we heard the whir of rotors—oh joy of technology! The Life-Flight helicopter circled, then set itself down, careful as a cat, on a rock jutting into the lake.

The kids wanted to pack up and meet me at the Kalispell hospital. "No," I insisted. "What good will that do?" I could call Bill to drive me home. It would be all right. As the helicopter lifted I saw the upturned faces of my children waving good-bye. I saw the Jewel Basin as a hawk might see it—the striated escarpments of the Swan Range rolling east toward the morning sun, the heavy green-black forests, the turquoise lakes. I looked down on the world, and it was beautiful.

ɕ   ɕ   ɕ

I cannot leave my story suspended in air. I will tell you another. It was July, one year later, and the twins and our friend M. C. decided we must celebrate the Fourth from the heights of Glacier Park. Steve, who was a singing waiter that summer at Many Glaciers Lodge in the park, would climb up to meet us on July 5 at Granite Park Chalet.

On the drive north we stopped at Polson, a small town on the shores of Flathead Lake where the Old-Time Fiddlers were having their annual contest. Fiddlers fat and tall, old and young, male and female practiced under trees on the high school lawn; other groups sipped beers and played favorites like "Dusty Miller" in the shade of Airstream trailers. In the gym a couple of oldsters dueled out versions of "The Orange Blossom Special." The fun stomped and whirled toward midnight. When we finally

motored into West Glacier, no one was guarding the gates.
The next morning we headed for Logan Pass (eleva-
tion 6,646 feet). This would be my first attempt at backpacking since my ankle had healed. We sweated under the
sun-gorged sky, but I wore my heavy hiking boots as well
as an elastic knee brace. Tourists thronged the Going-to-
the-Sun highway, and the first mile of the alpine trail to
Granite Park was strung with hikers in Ray-Bans. But as
the trail rose, the crowd thinned, and soon we were laughing in country so high there were no trees. We walked in
wildflowers and beargrass, cooled our feet in glacial waters,
climbed toward the snowy peaks. We spotted distant white
fluffs on scree—mountain goats. We met a man, his wife,
and their scared kids retreating from rumors of grizzlies.

The scare was legitimate. A ranger closed the trail
behind us as we passed. We would be the last folks allowed
into paradise. He told us to keep our eyes peeled for bear
sign, and we were rewarded. Here was an overturned log
shredded by great claws. Here was a steaming bear-sized
pile of scat.

Grizzlies, now threatened, once roamed the length of
North America. Their great size, humped swell of back
muscle, round ears and dished faces are unmistakable.
I have filmed grizzlies with my bear-man friend Doug
Peacock in Glacier Park's Apgar Range. Doug and I
bushwacked up brushy slopes thick with red-leafed huckleberry. I wanted to see a griz, but not to surprise one face-
to-face, so I called loudly to alert any browser with cubs
that foreigners were coming. When we reached Peacock's
secret viewing ground, a bald ridge he calls the Grizzly
Hilton, I wandered off across a dipping game trail. "Get
out of there!" Doug hissed. It seems I was blocking a major

grizzly highway—a road you want to avoid if you can. Peacock instructed me. If you see a griz, you must not run. A two-legged runner with a backpack looks like a wounded deer to a grizzly, triggering his prey-chasing instincts. Grizzlies are king of the food chain, not frightened by any living thing. Climb a tree if one is handy, for although black bears climb trees, grizzlies do not. If you are nuts for an adrenaline high, you might stand your ground, arms outstretched, head turned sideways in a subservient position. Avoid eye contact. Talk to the bear in a low voice. Or, more likely, curl up in a fetal position, arms protecting your head and neck. Play dead. The bear may paw you, tear flesh, puncture skin, but he's not likely to kill you.

Peacock likes getting close to bears. In the woods he eats grains and berries so he will smell like a bear. He smokes his clothes and gear over a campfire to get rid of giveaway odors. He talks to the bears and gives them names: Happy Bear, Alpha Bear, Yellow Bear. I prefer viewing grizzlies from afar, through heavy lenses. But no matter where I am, if I spot a griz on its own ground, I feel blessed. I hold my breath in a kind of prayer. Ah, wildness!

€   €   €

Granite Park Chalet is a stone pagoda rising above the trail like an Oriental mirage. It sits on a rocky plateau surrounded by glaciated peaks. Steve arrives before us and hikes down to relieve me of my pack. A group of Presbyterians on retreat from Missoula crowd the chalet's decks taking turns with 500-millimeter zoom lenses. We know the minister and his wife.

"There she is!" The silver-tipped grizzly sow ambles far below us on a grassy, pine-dotted slope. She grazes, unearthing roots, confident she is queen of the mountain. Her twin cubs are marked like Siamese cats with thick creamy coats, their ears, snouts, and tails tipped chocolate brown.

The sun casts long shadows from a pink-clouded sky. We walk the quarter mile to our campground, then hang our food a good distance from our bedding ground (the odds of survival in grizzly country are *much* better this way). We wash in a cold stream and cook our freeze-dried meal over the gas stove of a neighboring camper from Germany because our own old stove, dug out of the basement and untested, won't work. The air grows chill, and we warm ourselves with hot chocolate and Jack Daniel's.

At dawn I awake to a small circus. Andrew, shivering in boxer shorts, is hopping and swatting at a large dim creature. Alex doubles up in his down bag, consumed with giggles. M. C. wipes sleep from her eyes. Steve leaps out of his dream, ready to confront danger.

"What is it?" I cry. At such a moment, you think only of the great jowls of the beast.

"He's got my hat!"

"Who's got your hat?"

"The deer's got my hat."

After breakfast we find Andrew's Montana Grizzlies baseball hat in some brush. Sure enough, it is chewed, licked clean of the salt from his sweaty brow.

Deer crave salt. So do mountain goats. They also crave the minerals found in human urine. I have been followed around a campsite at Wall Lake in British Columbia by a half-tame mule deer waiting for me to take a leak. And

once, at Lake Ellen Wilson in Glacier, while my old buddy
Dave Nash took a nap and Bill and Pat and I splashed in
the icy waters, we heard a scream. We ran. Nash was rubbing his sunburned, balding brow. A molting old mountain
goat stood just out of harm's way.

"It licked me," said my wide-awake friend. "I felt this
rough thing on my head."

We go camping to be kissed by the wild. For a breath
of time we may think we are Eve or Adam in the garden
with beasts. I stand on mountains and seashores, or beneath
500-year-old redwoods, and I am humbled. It is not ecstasy
I seek, although ecstasy is always welcome, but the comfort-
ing knowledge that I am connected to the life around me.

What I crave is to be part of things, not greater than a
grizzly, not strong as a moose or swift as a rabbit. When I
return from the back country I'll stop at the nearest bar for
a tall, cool drink of water, then a gin and tonic or two. I
will step into my car, reborn at least until I get home.

When winter socks me in and cabin fever takes hold,
I'll invite friends over to view my slides. We will gather
around the fireplace, tell camping stories, bear stories, fish
stories — stories we need in order to survive in a world that
seems to be losing touch with what is primal.

Ride

Pack up your troubles
In your old kit bag,
And ride, ride, ride . . .

OLD RIDING SONG

The dudes who gather at the outfitter's roost could be the
cast for one of those ship-of-fools movies of the week:
a young plastic surgeon from Washington, D. C., his girlfriend and their pal, and Bill and me, a pair of middle-
aged writers. Also an elderly geologist, for our midsummer
horseback excursion into the Bob Marshall Wilderness is
to have a geological tilt.

We meet in an old farmhouse set amid a clump of
willows near Columbia Falls. The trip is a boondoggle
for me. My horse-trader companion Bill has made a swap:
our packer, who wants to be a writer, will take us for a
week's jaunt in barter for an editing job on his manuscript.
The packer's wife is a good ol' gal, chatty and game in
her red-checked gingham and blue jeans. After she cooks
us a breakfast of huckleberry pancakes, we pile into the
van for a dusty thirty-four-mile ride around Kicking
Horse Reservoir. The wrangler and a raw kid just graduated from outfitter's school have gone ahead with the
horses.

Packin' in, we call it, wilderness junkies riding the
spine of the Rockies every day, all summer long, from
Alberta to Arizona. On horses, of course, although it has
lately become fashionable for New-Agey transplants to
pack in on llamas, whose foreign scent has been known to
make horses go wild, like the scent of a lion or a grizzly
bear.

Some of our party wear battered Stetsons and high-
heeled cowboy boots, partaking of a Wild West romance in
which horses are the central icon. The more our world is
transformed by inanimate speed machines, the more we
yearn for the mythical creature of olden times—the Indian
pony, the buckaroo bronc. The placid mounts munching
hay by the horse trailers look up at us dudes with a weary
expression. These tourist-worn horses are a far cry from
anyone's icon. They size us up as if to say, "Here we go
again."

It's been a while since I've ridden, but I stroke
the nose of the chestnut mare who will carry me up the
mountain trail. In truth, I can't wait. Horse fever has never
left me.

⊏   ⊏   ⊏

After Dave and I settled on our small ranch, the first major
purchase we made was a quarter horse mare named
Almaree, who was with foal. In April the filly, Eustacia,
arose from her birthing place through a cover of wet snow,
two pointed red ears in the white meadow. Dave and I
loved to canter our horses over the pasture and into the
woods. But after he died I put away my second-hand saddle. I had become allergic to horses. If I stroked them or

brushed them my eyes began to itch. I had sneezing fits. My teary eyes would puff up so I could not see.

Bill grew up on horseback. From childhood, he rode a series of horses ranging from kids' ponies to cow horses to broncs. But when he realized he was not built to be a buckaroo—his legs were too short, his midsection too large—he switched to pickups and football, farming rather than herding. We had never before gone riding together.

Now, the outfitter brings Bill a tall old white gelding speckled with gray. Bill towers above the rest of the party. I have taken a couple of the antihistamines that will keep my allergy in check. Both of us are wearing hiking boots. His fleece jacket is red. Mine is the color of plums. We are bare-headed. Neither of us could pass the Marlboro Man test for western panache.

We ride seventeen miles the first day, a long trudge for greenhorns. We walk our horses along the South Fork of the Flathead River, the pines and firs so thick we can't see the mountains. The sun beats hot on our heads as powdery dust billows from under the pack train's hooves. My sweat merges with the smell of horse sweat. I try to fit my thighs and the small of my back to the sway and plod of my mare. The afternoon silence is broken by the chitchat of strangers, but never mind, we are escaping the commonplace as we ascend. The days file ahead like my trail companions— unknown, unhurried, unencumbered.

This is the charm of horsepacking. You do not carry your house on your back, like a snail. You do not have to labor each uphill step. If you go with an outfitter, you do not have to cook the meals or break the camps. You have put yourself into someone else's hands, and you are riding the back of a trained and graceful animal. You float above the earth, moving slow as a cloud, and your mind opens to the dream of place.

◘　◘　◘

Bob Marshall was a dreaming fellow, a rich Jewish New York boy who dreamed of being Lewis or Clark, a boy who worried that by the time he grew up there would be no more wilderness to explore. He became one of America's great foresters and worked his way up to chief of the Forest Service's Division of Recreation and Lands. By the time he died at thirty-eight of a heart attack in a Pullman car, he had logged 9,000 wilderness miles, hiking fifty miles or more a day in remote areas from Alaska's Brooks Range to the New Mexican desert. Marshall founded the Wilderness Society and dreamed of setting aside ten million acres in "regions sufficiently spacious that a person may spend at least a week or two of travel in them without crossing his own tracks."

Which is what we were up to in the 950,000 acres set aside in 1941 as America's largest wilderness area, dedicated to Bob Marshall. The Bob, as we Montanans familiarly call this oceanic highland of overthrust limestone reefs, glaciated peaks, cirque valleys, gravel-bedded trout rivers, and green pocket lakes, butts up to Glacier National Park and the Great Bear Wilderness to the north and sweeps south to the Scapegoat Wilderness. It is bounded on the west by the Swan Range and on the east by the abrupt, sheer and breathtakingly beautiful series of escarpments called the Rocky Mountain Front.

As we turn our horses toward White River Pass

through an open scrub forest of sub-alpine fir, Englemann spruce, and lodgepole pine we see the jumbled peaks of the Flathead Alps and our first upthrust reefs. The geologist points out inclines and synclines, folds, faults, slumps — words like poetry. I love the sound of those words but can't quite see through the layers of stone to abstract ideas about their formation. I am glad to get off my horse, stretch my saddle-sore legs.

I am a high-country addict, happy as a hawk every time I rise above the treeline — a famished hawk this day. At dusk we feast on barbecued steaks washed down with champagne — a surprise gift from the plastic surgeon, who had the wit to pack in a case.

ᴄ   ᴄ   ᴄ

Next day we wind ten miles along ridges, gullies, and old burns up to the packer's base camp near the headwaters of the White River. We learn to lead our steeds on downhill slopes and remount for the uphill treks. We canter into camp across a broad grassy cirque surrounded by mountains and bright with Indian paintbrush and lupine. We fall gratefully into our sleeping bags and look up to stars in a frosty black sky.

On the third day we set off for the Chinese Wall, a towering escarpment of white cliffs running from south to north that seems to split Montana in two. West of the wall are mountains, rivers, lakes, and forests; east lie the Great Plains, stretching all the way to Chicago. We tether our horses on a grassy ridge and climb up toward the rim. We look down from the white stone heights to a tawny sea of rolling grasslands where the Blackfeet tribe makes its home. Bill and I pose in dramatic postures for snapshots. In years to come we will study those photos and smile the secret knowing smiles of explorers.

Day four, rain. We sit in the grub tent, drink hot cocoa, read our novels, nap. When the rain stops, Bill and I rig up collapsible fly rods and fish the glass-clear White River for cutthroats. The trout are hard to catch from the grass-thick banks of the winding creek. We see them in pools, dappled with color, streaked red at the throat, darting and rare as pure mountain waters. Bill finally reels in a few ten-inchers and we fry them for dinner, sweet and crunchy fresh.

Day five, we have our adventure. Leaving the wrangler and his apprentice to relax in camp, the group rides toward Silvertip Mountain, where there are caves to explore. We park our horses and hike up a ridge. A cool wind blows, and soon we are hungry. As we devour ham sandwiches we see the wrangler galloping toward us. Bad news. The kid has been rodeoing the pack string; he had to prove he could ride the unridable horse, and the horse threw him, fell on his leg. The bone is sticking out of the skin. We are twenty-seven miles from any kind of help.

Luckily, the geologist is a ham-radio nut and has brought along a two-way. The packer and the plastic surgeon race down the mountain behind the wrangler. The rest of us scramble toward the ridge's highest point to send out our S.O.S. No answer from Spotted Bear Ranger Station; it's Sunday. At last the geologist makes contact with the sheriff in Libby, more than a hundred miles west as the crow flies, and the sheriff radios the hospital in Kalispell. By the time we reach camp the Life Flight whirlybird is circling. When the rodeo kid is lifted onto the litter he feels no pain. The plastic surgeon has drugs. Morphine, we guess, from the grin on the boy's face.

ㄷ　　ㄷ　　ㄷ

The next day our journey turns toward home. We ride over Larch Hill Pass and along the Continental Divide. Bill and I lead our horses across steep falls of scree. We scan the Wall Creek Cliffs, where shy grizzlies have been spotted, look for mountain sheep, see deer and the hind end of an elk. This is some of the wildest, most remote country in Montana. It is a haven for predators and prey that have been driven into these pockets of wilderness from shrinking and exploited habitat on every side.

Not many years ago, elk were dying out in the Bob Marshall ecosystem. The Boone & Crockett organization, dedicated to promoting hunting and trophy animals, bought land along the Sun River on the eastern slopes of the Rocky Mountain Front and set it aside as an elk preserve. With help from state and federal wildlife agencies, the herd revived. Once again the wilderness is a paradise for elk. And a paradise for the hunters who troop in every fall from Alabama, Oklahoma, Wisconsin, Pennsylvania.

As we ride downhill, the pine forest encloses us again. I begin to feel claustrophobic, depressed. I do not want to return to my sheltered valley. I want to stay high as the raw kid on what Bob Marshall called "the perfect aesthetic experience," vast panoramas "on a scale so overwhelming as to wipe out the ordinary meaning of dimensions."

My "ordinary dimension" is pretty wild, pretty fair, but it cannot compete with mountains on top of the world. It would take months to explore the Bob Marshall, learn its paths, feel its weather, study the habits of birds, fish, beaver, and bear. There are lakes to raft, peaks to climb, limits of endurance to discover.

"I don't want to go home," I whine. Here, I will never be sated. Like the bald eagle lifting on air currents around Pentagon Peak, all I want is to ride, ride, ride.

Wallowa

In the remote northeastern corner of Oregon there is a
sacred land to which I sometimes go. I drive U. S. 12 south
and west from Missoula over Lolo Pass into Idaho, retracing backwards the 1877 escape route of the bands of Nez
Perce Indians called renegade.

The Nez Perce exodus consisted of women, children,
old people, and 2,000 horses under the care of Peace Chief
Joseph, while war chiefs Looking Glass and Ollocut led a
small force of two hundred warriors. Although the rest of
the Nez Perce had agreed to become Christians and to
live on an arid reservation along the Clearwater River in
Idaho at Lapwai, Joseph's people refused to give up their
traditional religious practices or sell their tribal homes
and hunting grounds in the Wallowa Mountains. Rather
than be relocated by the U. S. government so that
white homesteaders could safely claim their bounteous
Oregon land, Joseph's people chose to run and to fight
if necessary.

In a series of skirmishes along the Clearwater, then
eastward into Montana over the Bitterroot range, the Nez
Perce led the U. S. cavalry on a five-month cat-and-mouse
chase. At almost every step they outmaneuvered the white
militia and horse soldiers led by General Howard. Across
the nation tabloid readers followed their exploits, many

rooting for the outnumbered Indians like fans cheering an underdog team in the World Series.

Sometimes the chase was comic, as in the Fort Fizzle escapade, where the Nez Perce slipped through dense forests up Lolo Pass while the bushwhacking army built elaborate barricades. Other times the chase was tragic. At the battle of the Big Hole, during an army ambush near what is now called Chief Joseph Pass, General Howard's and General Gibbons's soldiers suffered thirty-six dead, forty wounded. The Nez Perce lost almost ninety lives, most of the casualties women and children.

The non-treaty Nez Perce fled south and east, continuing to outsmart the generals through Montana and into newly-established Yellowstone National Park. Then they turned north over the plains, and when they reached the rounded slopes of the Bear Paw Mountains, they stopped to rest and hunt buffalo for winter provisions, knowing General Howard was two days behind them. The bedraggled, much-diminished Nez Perce people thought they could rest safely just forty miles from the Canadian border, where Sioux Chief Sitting Bull promised protection. They thought their 600-mile odyssey had ended. But they were wrong. They did not know General Howard had sent a message to alert Colonel Miles. On that bitter, snow-blown night, the first day of October, 1877, Colonel Miles and his horsemen rode down from the north, surprising the slumbering camp.

"I felt the end coming," said Yellow Wolf. "All for which we had suffered lost! Thoughts came of the Wallowa, where I grew up. Of my own country when only Indians were there. Of tipis along the bending river. Of the blue, clear lake, wide meadows with horse and cattle herds.

From the mountain forests, voices seemed calling . . ."

After five freezing days of battle, with most of his warriors dead in the trenches, Chief Joseph surrendered. The translated speech he made is one of the most famous oratories in American history. "I am tired of fighting," said Joseph. "Our chiefs are killed. Looking Glass is dead. Toohoolhoolzote is dead. . . . The little children are freezing to death. My people, some of them, have run away to the hills, and have no blankets, no food. . . . I want to look for my children and see how many of them I can find. . . . Hear me, my chiefs! I am tired. My heart is sick and sad. From where the sun now stands I will fight no more forever."

ᴄ ᴄ ᴄ

Fighting is far from my mind this sun-shot morning as I wind west into Idaho through elk and mountain-goat country on cliffs above the rapid-strewn Lochsa River. I speed past Jerry Johnson Hot Springs. The last time I hiked in, Mount Saint Helens had just blown her top, and the pines had been dusted white with volcanic ash. Today every needle shines. Sweaty and bottom-sore from driving, I stop where the Lochsa flows into the Clearwater River for a quick dip, then refresh my taste buds with a ritual slice of huckleberry pie at the Syringa Cafe.

Highway 12 unfolds through Nez Perce Reservation towns and along the once-burgeoning steelhead fisheries of the Clearwater. I roll past Nez Perce National Historic Park in Spalding, named for Presbyterian missionaries Henry and Eliza Spalding, who in the mid-1800s had labored to convert the Nez Perce. I do not stop, because I have walked these grounds before. I have visited the

museum, and I know the bleak history of this place by
heart, having written a screenplay about Eliza Spalding
and her companion, Narcissa Whitman, who was massacred by the Indians she came to "save."

Eliza and Narcissa were the first white women to tra-
verse the Rockies. Although I hold no truck with their
zealot's mission—the boring urge to make everyone be like
you—I admire their courage and feel a sisterly envy. I,
myself, will never realize the true adventures they experienced. I will never be first in unknown territory, except in
my imagination, which is not good enough. Still, the twen-
tieth century has its advantages. I think of bouncing in a
wagon bed through this hot dry rocky trough. My Subaru
has no air-conditioning, and my mind begins to melt as the
wind blisters in through open windows, but I'm covering
ground at seventy miles per hour.

In hundred-degree heat the smoking, stinking stacks
of the pulp mill in Lewiston seem a mirage from hell. I
breathe more easily as I cross the Snake River into Washington State, turning south on Highway 129, which in
another forty miles will become Oregon Highway 3. The
road is a plunging series of switchbacks into the gorge of the
Grande Ronde River. This isolated stretch must be driven
in daylight. If you are lucky (as I was once), you may see a
mountain lion perched on a red bluff. Now I pounce on my
brakes to avoid a mule deer and her twin spotted fawns.

The air cools as I climb a piney plateau that rises to
4,693 feet near the northern border of Chief Joseph's land.
The Oregon town of Enterprise is the gateway to the Wallowa Valley, and there a traveler will find some not-too-
fancy motels and restaurants. Stop at The Book Loft and
pick up a copy of Alvin Josephy's *The Nez Perce Indians and*

the Opening of the Pacific Northwest. In this Bancroft Prize-winning history, you can read about Lewis and Clark being fed and sheltered by the Nez Perce. You can find excerpts from the diaries of Eliza Spalding and Narcissa Whitman. And, if you have the heart, you can follow a day-to-day account of Chief Joseph's tragic flight. There is no better guide to this country.

Six miles south of Enterprise, Highway 3 dead-ends at a glacial moraine that forms a natural dam at the base of Wallowa Lake just beyond the tiny town of Joseph. I scramble up the moraine and look out over the green ranching valley that spreads below the Wallowa Mountains. I imagine the Nez Perce tipi rings that Yellow Wolf described: women in buckskins gathering firewood, cooking, doing the chores of daily life; children bathing in the lake; herds of spotted Appaloosa horses. I imagine those horses running in tall grass, but what I see is fenced pastures, boxy houses, fields speckled with black Angus cattle.

Across Wallowa Lake are the jutting spires of the 220,000-acre Eagle Cap Wilderness Area, white with perpetual snows. An ice-cooled breeze zips down from the heights and makes me shiver. I watch the orange sun dip beyond mountaintops into the depths of a purple, fist-shaped thunderhead.

I could end my day by driving one of the back roads into the wilderness and camping out. Next morning I could go horsepacking or trekking with llamas to a few of the more than sixty alpine lakes that offer some of the best trout fishing in the Northwest. I could even attempt to climb the Matterhorn (9,000 feet), which is striped with blue-veined marble and shelters bighorn sheep. But I have other purposes.

Along the access road that borders Lake Wallowa's
shore, I pass a monument dedicated to Chief Joseph. I stop
there for a moment of tribute, then enter a state park
where campgrounds and motels border waters shadowed
by the dark mountains. I know at pavement's end there is a
trail into the highlands. I will walk through a ponderosa
forest on a cushion of fallen needles, each step releasing the
heady perfume of dust and pine. This day's travel will end
in solitude on a dusky cliff above a waterfall.

      ◨   ◨   ◨

I have come to the Wallowas this July to participate in
some western culture at the Fishtrap Gathering, held an-
nually in a ramshackle Methodist camp. I will join other
aspiring writers under a blue tent-top for workshops, read-
ings, and discussions with the likes of Ursula LeGuin, Bill
Kittredge, Jim Welch, and Terry Tempest Williams. Also
agents and editors from New York, and our resident hosts
and old friends, Alvin and Betty Josephy.
    Culture, however, can wait a day, for I am going to go
exploring. After a good night's sleep, I meet up with Alvin
Josephy's eldest daughter, Diane Peavey, a couple of her
Idaho friends, and my Utah sister in adventure, Terry
Williams. We pack a lunch and leave the cool highlands for
a thirty-mile descent toward the bottomlands of the Snake
River in the Hell's Canyon National Recreation Area.
Diane's jeep winds down, down, down a rutted track into
Imnaha Canyon—a world of sagebrush, rock terraces, and
hot red sun, a territory as different as you can get from the
green pastures where we began our journey.
    Inside Imnaha Canyon we must make a decision. We

can take the rough two-track to Hat Point and peer down almost 7,000 feet to the desert floor of Hell's Canyon, which is 1,000 feet deeper than the Grand Canyon. Vistas are nice for tourists, but we want to be involved with the interior life of the country. So we take the other road, descending through flowering ranchlands along willow-laced streams that shelter deer and small game.

About a slow hour's ride down the 4 x 4 trail to the Snake, we stop at the Josephy family's favorite swimming hole on Cow Creek. We are more hot than hungry, and in this huge desert canyon we five women are the only humans in sight. We strip off our clothes. There is a pool of crystal water I must dive into, sandy bottoms that do not hurt tender feet. Terry lies half submerged, coats her bare body with oozing sand. I follow her example. I feel my skin tighten as the sand dries and cakes. Later, we will body-surf the rapids, climb cliffs, eat turkey sandwiches, garden tomatoes, and green grapes, and drink bottles of sparkling white wine. Then, full-bellied and river-washed, we will snooze in the slanting light of the afternoon sun.

My friends and I cavort like the daughters of Eve we in fact are. In this secluded temple of pink rock and coarse sands, we are as free and lost to self-consciousness as nymphs. Only ghosts of the Nez Perce keep us company. I believe they are friendly ghosts. Women who once bathed in this pool with their brown naked children. Sun-mother elders who smile with benevolence at our snake-like shedding of old skins.

Chief Joseph's Nez Perce made their homes in the canyons of the Imnaha and the Snake, in the meadows and mountains called Eagle Cap and Wallowa. Summers they hunted the highlands, winters they descended into the sheltering warm canyons and lived amid an abundance of fish and game. It was their paradise then, and at this moment it is ours. We must take care to protect our wild gardens. The renegade bands were right: this is a land worth fighting for.

Fishing the Tundra

Tundra, a Russian word derived from the Lapp *tundar*
and akin to the Finnish *tunturi,* means "bare Arctic hill-
scape." The sound of it is drumsong. Say it—tundra,
tundra, tundra.

The actuality is a thin and spongy skin of life over
stone, over permafrost. The tundra is red this Alaskan
morning in September from the turned leaves of cranberry
brush and blueberry brush. It is yellow grass and brown
ferns, lichens and green moss. The tundra is a tapestry pat-
terned with swatches of black spruce, sun-gold with aspen
and cottonwood, etched with caribou trails and the accom-
panying wolf trails like roads on a prehistoric map. In June,
says our pilot, the tundra is green and smooth as a golf
course. In July it is speckled blue and white with wildflowers and the purple monkshood.

Dipping low in our Cessna 185 like a raptor eyeing
prey we see caribou scattered on the open ground in groups
of three or twelve or fifty. We see the animals clear and
simple as sacred beasts in cave paintings, their antlers like
scrolls from time immemorial; and among the firs or in the
swampy pond grass we see the massive dark and solitary
moose before rut, the immense racks of the bulls gleaming
like beacons, saying "come to me, I am the greatest."

The tundra is running with waters. And the waters are running with fish. That is why I am here, to fish. But it is the air that transports me. In my next life I will be a bush pilot or an Arctic swan. The swans are pure white on glacial ponds, white vessels on the lakes and the rivers that lace this landscape from the mountains to the sea.

"It's a land of weeping mountains," says my laconic guide, who is also our pilot. I'm taken aback by this poetic outburst, but he is correct. The volcanoes that rise above the tundra hold blue glaciers in their summits, and the glaciers weep waterfalls—white water against black stone—and the waters converge into fast-running clear streams, which converge again into the broad rivers that feed the great salmon fisheries of Bristol Bay.

ᴄ   ᴄ   ᴄ

Alaska is a world drawn in on itself—a kingdom of men, it seemed as I sat in the bar at the Anchorage airport waiting for the commuter flight to Dillingham. I sipped my beer, picked at my popcorn. I was surrounded by burly, jolly men in fishing hats and hunting vests, their overstuffed camo duffel bags piled beside rods and gun cases. The few women in the bar gave me comfort. There was a dark-skinned mother with two children, an elderly lady in tweeds sitting with her suited husband, an Inuit girl engrossed in her book.

I was excited and a bit scared, for I was going fishing with guides. In Montana I usually walk the banks of the Big Blackfoot with my shepherd dogs, birdwatching, swimming, absorbing light from the river. In years past I also walked beside rivers while my husband and little boys threw out their lines. I was the person who untangled monofilament for five-year-olds, cooked the trout but hated to kill them. In Montana I had always been the Woman Who Walks Along. But my husband was twenty years dead, my sons grown and gone, my companion a golfer. I was going to have to cast a fly under expert eyes, a prospect that made my stomach turn and my hands shake.

A soft, cool rain was falling when a young man named Steve picked me up at Dillingham Airport. We drove twenty-four miles on a dirt road along the Wood River to the parking area of the native village at Lake Aleknagik. He slung my overnight bag and Kelty day-pack into an open motorboat and offered me a khaki slicker.

"You must be a traveling lady," said Steve with a broad grin. "The biggest mistake most folks make is too much gear."

Mission Lodge is the dominant structure along the lake, set in dark firs with its back to the mountains, accessible only by boat or plane or cars barged across the waters to the native village and the few roads on the far shore. Its long row of third-floor dormered windows reflected the last light of dusk, and the lower floors glowed warm yellow. We pulled up to a dock where seaplanes were tethered like sleeping birds.

After a dinner of filet mignon and shrimp (every Mission Lodge dinner features two tasty entrees) Mary and Jim Broady, who are managers and part owners, would explain to me that the place had once been a Seventh Day Adventist boarding school, hence the name. In 1951 the church bought an old cannery, floated it up the Wood River on a barge, and set it up as a Christian school for the village children. In 1965 they erected the building that houses the main lodge. By 1974, when the state of Alaska built new

nondenominational public schools in Dillingham and
Aleknagik, the mission school had folded. It remained
empty until 1984, when Jim Broady and his partner, Dale
DePriest, bought it, restored and redecorated it, and
opened their wilderness fishing enterprise.

That evening about thirty people gathered around the
free-standing fireplace in the paneled living room. They
clustered in armchairs and on sofas, leaned against the bar.
Half were guests, the rest guides, waitresses, pilots. It
seemed a family gathering, and in many ways it was, for
this was the end of the season, and two guides had invited
their folks. To make matters more confusing, several of the
staff were married to each other, and a few guests were old
pals of the Broadys, come back to the lodge for the fourth
or fifth year, bringing a soldier son, an eighty-two-year-old
southern uncle.

Dressed in jeans and sweatsuits, moccasins and plaid
shirts, I could not tell the guests from the staff, which is
how the Broadys like it—informal. At one point I noticed
a group of men talking intently at one of the long dining
tables with boss-man Jim. They were the pilots and guides
deciding who would fish where the next day, basing their
calls on weather, the fishing desires of particular guests,
and reports of the past day's fishing: Where were the rainbows biting? How far would you have to go for silver
salmon? Which rivers were high, too muddy?

A few moments later a compact fellow with a thin
blond mustache came up to me. "I'm Dan," he said.
"You'll be coming with me tomorrow. We're going to
go lake-hopping, see the lay of the land."

 ◖   ◖   ◖

The land lay swathed in ground fog that first morning, the fog diminishing as we flew north. To the west rose jagged peaks of the Wood River Mountains, pink in the morning sun, a few ice-blue glaciers nestled in 6,000 foot summits. To the east the bare tundra sprawled like a prairie. We passed over a series of stair-step lakes joined by brief, swift stretches of the Wood River: Lakes Nerka, Beverley, Nuyakuk, Chauekuktuli, Chickuminuk, Upnuk, and Nishlik. Lake Aleknagik makes its bed near sea level, but at the high end Lake Nishlik sits at 1200 feet.

As the crow flies we traveled some seventy miles, but we did not fly like a crow. We dipped and banked, tracking moose. We scouted high ground for brown bears, the Alaskan relative of the American grizzly, a more carnivorous variety that thrives on salmon runs, mainly sockeye. About 7,000 brown bears roam this region from the mountains to the coast, the largest concentration in Alaska. Finally, under a luminous blue sky, we dropped to the north end of Lake Chikuminuk and pulled ashore next to a flat-bottomed motorboat owned by the lodge.

"We don't worry about thieves," said Dan. "Where could they go, except down the lake?"

A person has to readjust her thinking when she is sixty miles from a house, a road. In this unpeopled Alaskan community, pilot/guides are like itinerant cowboys working one outfit one year, another the next. Everyone knows them and their rigs.

We fished from the boat with spinning gear. I launched my line with its weighted, glittering lure as far as I could, let it sink a moment, and slowly reeled it in. My boat mates were friends from Dan's hometown in Minnesota, a banker and his wife. The man was more hunter than fisherman, and when he spotted a bull moose on a brushy hillside a few hundred yards away he decided he'd go tracking while the rest of us played our lines. A pair of Arctic loons landed on the lake. They swam low on the water, elegant necks arched.

I finally caught a couple of Arctic char and a mid-sized lake trout while wading along a small peninsula. Not confident enough to slip the unbarbed hooks from the fishes' mouths, I asked Dan do the unhooking. Although the state of Alaska allows daily and possession limits on various species of native fish, the sporting way is catch and release. It's environmentally correct: let the fish go to reproduce. My philosophy is predatory. It says kill what you catch (except if its a baby or a female fat with eggs) and keep only what you can eat. I have never looked kindly on playing catch-me-if-you-can with a living being just for the thrill of it, just for the skill. But I was going to give the game a try, see if I, like Eric, like my friends, would become addicted.

Later, fishing the other end of Chikuminuk at the mouth of a gravel-bedded stream, I hooked and released char after fat char, their golden bodies spotted silver, a few turned spawn red on their underbellies. We ate two of the largest (about twenty-one inches) for lunch, grilled in foil over coals with lemon, butter, and onion. The meat of the char is red as salmon, but milder. What can surpass the satisfaction of sitting on a wilderness shore, eating your fresh-caught fish, and washing it down with beer?

E   E   E

The second day would be my fishing marathon. We ate at seven from a breakfast buffet featuring such forbidden pleasures as biscuits and gravy, waffles, sausage and bacon, and for those disciplined enough to abstain, dry cereals, oatmeal, and fruit. We pulled on our neoprene waders and boots in the furnace room where we had hung them to dry, gathered our rods, polarized glasses, chapstick, finger-less gloves, binoculars and cameras, and trooped down to the dock.

Six of us climbed into a Beaver, the 1940s utility float plane you see in movies, sturdy enough to haul lumber, drilling pipe, or small boats on top of its pontoons. We were flying only twenty miles to the one-and-a-half mile Agulukpak River, which joins Lake Beverley to Lake Nerka. It was a popular spot, and the two motorboats of our party had to share the fish-rich river with four other boats from other lodges.

Our guide tied a salmon-egg imitation to my fly line, weighted it with a lead shot and attached a pink foam indi-cator that works like a bobber. After a few miscasts and tangled lines, I learned to make the proper abbreviated cast, and as we drifted downstream my indicator dipped. I set my hook and netted a fighting rainbow.

All day we would drift down the clear, rapid river, its bottom red with spawning sockeye. We would catch and release Dolly Varden, arctic char, and grayling by the dozen. When the water became too rapid to float, our guide would fire up the motor, and back to the lake we'd go for another run. I stood in the prow. I cast until my right arm was sore. I learned that hooked char whirl like a corkscrew; that the sail-finned grayling are a lighter pull; that if you think you've got hold of a log, you've snagged a sockeye; and that elusive rainbows, leaping and running, will give the most satisfaction.

We lunched at a small cabin on a bluff at the entrance

to the river, the inhabitants two college students from the East who worked for Wood-Tikchik State Park, the largest state park in the United States. "Did you know all these lakes are in our state park?" asked the young woman. She was taking a survey.

"Yes," I nodded. "Do you have an outhouse?"

She pointed me up the bluff. I looked for bears feeding on sockeye along the shore, but saw nothing but gulls. Although others had seen bears here the day before, and that evening our pilot would almost run into a brown bear at the mouth of the river, I never spotted one except from the air. The outhouse had a gorgeous view. I pulled down my waders and sat serenely on the throne, studying cloud shadows on the glassy lake, the blue and purple snow-decked mountains that embraced it.

On the last run, our guide pulled into an eddy near a small feeder stream. I wanted to catch a grayling on a dry fly to honor Bill Kittredge's father, an old sportsman I had loved, who drove to Alaska at age eighty-seven for that purpose only. He never caught his fish, but I did. The grayling was fourteen inches, with indigo iridescent streaks under its silvery scales.

"Oscar, this one's for you," I said as the freed fish fled into a sun-dappled riffle.

       ⊑   ⊑   ⊑

On the third day it rained. I shivered under the dripping sky. A seasoned pilot from Lake Tahoe named Al, who looks like Robert Ryan in his waning days, noticed. "Ya know," he said. "This wet climate's what fish like. Sunny days are dull days for fish."

We flew northeast up the wide Nushagak River,
which joins with the Wood River above Dillingham and
dumps its fish-laden waters into Bristol Bay. We flew over
native villages, over fish camps and Aleutian willow fishing weirs that looked to me like Ferris wheels. Two caribou watched us land next to a gravel bar at the lodge's
fishing camp.

Chris, a college-age guide who lives in a tent with a
wooden floor and a gas stove, greeted us with hot coffee.
We pulled on our rain gear and in two open boats motored
down a side channel toward what Chris gleefully calls
"the Aquarium." We anchored along the downstream
bank near the channel's juncture with the high, brown
Nushagak. Reeds poked out of a deep green pool, the
waters turning opaque and black under a canopy of
dripping alders. A family of five otters poked their sleek,
round-eared heads up across the stream, eyeing us curi-
ously before they dove to their own fishing.

Chris had a fly rod ready for me, set up steelhead
fashion, with monofilament line. He tied on a wet fly,
an Egg-Sucking Leech, known as "the lawyer's lure."

"Not much dry fly fishing up here," he explained. "Not
like Montana." The rivers were too rich with eggs and fry
and insect hatches too sporadic for the trout to be bothered
with surface feeding. Chris added a cluster of weights to the
line so it would bounce across the bottom, where the fish
feed. Again I caught Dollies, char, and grayling, but lost at
least three rainbows before I hooked the daddy. I played
him for ten minutes, until my arms got tired.

"She's got a big one," Chris shouted to the more
accomplished fishermen in the other boat. "A six-pounder."

After lunch the rainbows refused our wet flies, so we

switched rods and tried casting with big pink froglike plugs, which is how they fish king salmon. The guides motored slowly upstream, holding against the current as we cast. Soon everyone's rods were bent with big trout. I got a serious bite, and with the motion of the boat keeping my line taut, we pulled into shore. It seemed like cheating, but I landed an eight-pound rainbow worthy of a photograph.

Chris cradled him in the water, and I placed my hands under his belly. He was a fat fellow, his red-streaked sides battered and scarred. Large rainbows with their bullet heads will ram a female sockeye to jar her eggs loose and feast on them. To protect their spawn, sockeyes will attack the rainbows. This was an old warrior, and we let him go to fight again.

The light was green in the heavy rain, green all day and getting darker. I had caught a trout to brag on, but I was tired, wet, and suddenly chilled. It was time to go home. I couldn't wait to get back to the lodge, pour myself a tumbler of Jack Daniel's, and soak in the outdoor Jacuzzi before dinner.

⌐   ⌐   ⌐

On my last day the weather turned cold and bright. The dogs at the lodge, especially the old malamute, did a dog-dance of joy in expectation of snow. We flew 130 miles southeast over Bristol Bay and the Gas Rocks volcanic region of the Alaskan Peninsula in the direction of Kodiak Island. As our Cessna bucked and plunged in the updrafts of a mountain pass running with waterfalls, I caught sight of the deep blue Pacific Ocean. The pure beauty of head-lands and beaches backed against the red and gold tundra and a range of glaciated black mountains made me feel high as a seabird in flight.

We slid to water in a secret spot that Jim Broady calls his Wonder Pond and walked across the vivid tundra toward a gravelly stream where we would find silver salmon. I fished with a spinning rod again, jigging fluorescent green and pink plastic lures that looked like squid from another planet. We could see the dark shapes of a dozen silvers in a large pool where the stream curved against a rock cliff on its two-mile run toward the sea. Spawning salmon do not feed, but they will snap up any bright intruder that threatens their grounds, and they were on the fight. My fishing companion was a retired stockbroker from New England, an accomplished fisherman who casts a mean wet fly. We fished in holy silence broken only by my calls for help as I caught a salmon and tried to release it, or snagged my line on the rocky ledge. But when another group from our lodge came downstream to fish our spot, the place lost its allure.

One Florida developer with permed hair dyed yellow had killed his two-salmon limit and asked if he could keep the ten-pounder I had just landed. Although I had planned to return home with my fresh catch, I decided to be a sport. The silver run was so poor that year that it was bad form to keep any. "No," I said. "This fish is going to breed if I have anything to do with it."

"You know," said our pilot/guide Bill, who is an old Alaska hand known for his fiddle playing and derring-do, "I hate to thump a hen. Those eggs'll be thousands of little silvers. Let the fish go and maybe she'll help 'em come back."

I handed him my rod and climbed the bank, heading

for high ground where you could see the ocean. I had walked twenty yards, clumsy in my neoprene waders, when I came face to face with a red fox. The fox was large as a coyote, tall on slender legs, his red tail ringed white at the base, his red ears pointed at me. After a long moment he sauntered to a clump of alder brush, sat down as if I couldn't see him, and peeked around it like an inquisitive child.

The afternoon sun glinted off whitecaps on the Pacific. A small wind blew aspen leaves onto the silver stream where salmon spawned, and ruffed the yellow grass. I walked in red-leafed brush, and the red fox watched.

If only I had a tent, I thought, a sleeping bag and a cache of food. I would be quiet and canny as the fox. I would talk to the magpies and roam beaches with gulls. Maybe I would see a brown bear and not be afraid, because the bear would be full of fish and not interested in the likes of me. I felt small and insignificant, in proper scale amid the paradisal life of this tundra. I could make a home here, I dreamed, at least until the snow flies.

Andalusia, Again

What is the deepest loss you have suffered?
If drinking is bitter, change yourself to wine.

RAINER MARIA RILKE

"Spain," said the Wyoming poet Jim Galvin, "is only
Nevada with castles." Galvin was trying to persuade us to
stay in the misty valleys of Umbria, his adopted country
of choice. But Bill and I were not persuaded. Nevada
with castles would be just fine. This was Bill's first trip to
Europe, and in our rented red Renault we slipped and
skidded into Spain from Perpignan over a pass covered
with a foot of wet January snow.

A western American will recognize the emotional
geography of his imagination in Spain. "Should have
listened to Galvin," Bill grumbled. Stuck in the mountains
in what the radio said was a once-in-ten-years snow was
an experience we could have any winter day in Montana.
So we sped south as fast as we could on brand new black
asphalt freeways. We slowed our pace as we approached
Andalusia over barren Moorish landscapes fragrant with
oranges and lemons from the huge agribusiness orchards
that surround Valencia and Murcia. Whitewashed chimneys of troglodyte cave dwellings rose from stone villages
like fairy tale mushrooms; and when we arrived at the

heights of Granada's Alhambra, bedding like pashas in a palace among the gardens, we were Dorothy and the Lion in the Emerald City. This was not Nevada at all.

The Alhambra had been home to Islamic kings in the late fourteenth century, and travelers reported the royal hilltop was an embodiment of grace built by angels, not men. Arabian poets sang in the courtyards and philosophers discoursed. When Spanish Christians under Queen Isabella stormed Granada in 1492, the last shah of the Nasrid dynasty, Abu Abdallah, retreated across the Mediterranean. "Weep like a woman," his mother told him, "you who have not defended your kingdom like a man."

I walked in the Alhambra's tiled gardens among cool shaded pools and breathed the ghost-scent of harem roses. On marble terraces stray cats stretched in winter's thin sunlit air. Granada had been the most advanced planned Islamic city of ancient days. Later it became a university town for Catholic scholars. And in the turmoil of the Spanish Civil War, homeboy Garcia Lorca, the radical, gay poet whose blood-red vision of the interior life of Andalusia had so entranced me, was assassinated by Franco's minions in a nearby village.

I came to Granada expecting to be overwhelmed by memories, for I had been there a quarter century before, with Dave and Dick Hugo, and Eric and Steve when they were just boys. But all I could remember of that distant time was a dreamlike vista of aquamarine fountains and white-blossoming almond trees framed by an arched portal like lace carved in stone.

◧   ◧   ◧

From Granada Bill and I drove toward the Mediterranean on a back road marked "scenic" on our tourist map. We entered highlands newly planted with seedling pines in parallel rows to the horizon. Once these gray coastal ranges had been swathed in green forests and running with deer, but centuries of wood-gathering peasants and their herds of goats have denuded the land. I wondered if my logged-over Montana hills are fated to follow this model, if the intricate chaos of all remaining natural systems will be reduced to a machine-driven geometry of monocultures designed to sustain the cancer of human populations.

Our little red car plunged down the sheer-walled Sierra de Almijara on a slalom-course road through blooming almond orchards, along red cliffs green-dotted with olive trees into a canyon thick with groves of grapefruit and avocados. This semi-tropical paradise was more garden than plantation, warm and welcoming in its variety and smallness, its connection to the irregular vagaries of earth and water. We lunched under a hot January sun at an inn at Otivar, the deck jammed with red-jowled Brits eating roasted chickens for Sunday dinner.

Driving along the only unspoiled coast we were to see that day, we arrived at the small city of Nerja, where I wintered with Dave and the boys in 1968 when the twins were only two months old. Except for new white villas cluttering the hills, Nerja was the place I remembered. Bill parked in a square bordering the Mediterranean, and like a homing pigeon I went directly to the house on the Fisherman's Calle that Dave and I had rented.

I stood in the polished stone foyer where a line of stout peasant women had surprised me at dawn so many years ago, each one arguing in dialect I could barely decipher that she alone would be the best maid in town. I remembered awakening to flamenco songs sung by *muchachas* as they washed the stone streets in front of white houses with barred windows. Shopkeepers had called me La Franchesa because I spoke lame, market Spanish with a French accent, French the only foreign language embedded in my brain.

The makeshift outdoor movie screen outside our patio wall had been torn down, but the small crescent beach below the cliffhanging street was the same. One sunny January day I had put on my two-piece bathing suit to go swimming. Dave followed a few moments later. Soon he was shouting and waving, knee-deep in the sea, holding my towel. "Get out! Don't ask. Get out right now!" As he rushed me away, Dave pointed toward several shabby smiling men of the town who sat on their heels behind the shells of beached fishing boats. It seems they had gathered to masturbate while I leaped unknowing in the gentle salt waves. It was on this fishermen's beach that Dave realized something drastic was wrong with his heart. He lost his breath from walking fast. He feared that the pain sweeping into his left arm when he lifted our chubby babies was angina.

Now, nearly twenty years after Dave's death, I touched the weathered stone walls of our house and wept for the sweet terrors of youth. Like the women of Troy, like Achilles tearing his hair for slain Petrocles, I was weeping for myself.

◘   ◘   ◘

The first time I came to Andalusia, David was thirty-four and I was thirty-one. We had traveled from England to Spain with our four boys—the twins red and squalling. We hadn't expected twins when we embarked for Europe that September. What I wanted was a dark-haired daughter to keep me company in a houseful of men. I would never have gone abroad if I knew twins were coming, but my Montana doctor could hear only one baby heartbeat, and I refused to have an x-ray until my eighth month. By then we were living in a London suburb and I had grown so huge I was afraid I'd give birth to a monster. After the babies emerged twelve minutes apart on Thanksgiving eve, I became a skinny shadow of myself with hair falling out, teeth going bad. My English doctor, Mr. Butcher, ordered me not to nurse my ravenous litter.

Dave was not well either. He had frightened me in England by going comatose with a bad case of the flu. Then, one snowy afternoon, while playing fox-and-geese with Eric and Steve in the backyard of our sixteenth-century Amersham cottage, he passed out. Common sense told us to go home to safety, but this was Dave's sabbatical, the trip we had been planning for a year, and common sense could go fly a kite.

Raw and yearning, poor and full of romantic notions, we rented a tiny trailer on the Costa Brava, north of Barcelona, attached it to the Land Rover station wagon we had bought in England, and headed southwest along the Mediterranean. The twins had diarrhea. They took turns crying at night. We enlisted Eric and eleven-year-old Steve into the arduous work of babysitting. Dave and I took turns at the wheel, so hair-trigger exhausted we fought until my eyes were red with perpetual tears.

We made our way along the coast to Portugal, looking for the perfect Andalusian fishing village where we could be artists in exile. We camped in orange groves and on deserted beaches, and no matter how remote the spot, we were shadowed by Franco's Guardia Civil. The national police wore tri-cornered hats, rode motorcycles, and carried machine guns. *"Vigilancia,"* one of them said to me as I sneaked out of our trailer to take a pee. He was guarding us, but from what? Dave and I figured the word was out we were drug dealers expecting a shipment from North Africa, and the babies were an elaborate disguise. Laughter revived us.

Finding no perfect place, we backtracked to Nerja, the only suitable town we had seen, thirty miles east of Malaga. It was known for its stalactite-hung caves and its *Balcon de Europa*, a tiled, palm-lined belvedere where promenaders enjoy a 280-degree view of the picture-book coast. Garcia Lorca's house stood kitty-corner from ours, and we kept company with the family of an Irish writer who lived down the block. Dick Hugo came to visit from southern Italy. He passed the month drinking to excess and courting English girls at the *parador* where he roomed.

One Sunday in February we decided to make a pilgrimage to Ronda in honor of the great German poet Rainer Maria Rilke, who had lived there in 1912 and 1913. After Bloody Marys on the deck of an ugly new hotel in Marbella, we were tipsy as we drove up the coastal range on a rutted jeep road, Hugo reciting "My Buddy," his latest and most nonsensical poem, from the front seat of our Land Rover:

Andalusia, Again

This then buddy is the blue routine.
You chased a fox one noon.
She hid in a golden rain.
You ran through the gold until
a rainy chill.
If that's it buddy it's a bleak routine.
What happened to you there
may never happen again.

◪　　◪　　◪

Bill and I drove into the night along the overbuilt, crummy
Costa del Sol. We were touring Spain in a flying hurry,
having lost three days of our thirty-day trip during the
Perpignan snowstorm. Next time, we decided, we will settle
a while in Andalusia. We will bed down in Antequera,
a town so old even the Romans called it Ancient City, and
spend a day exploring the three dolmens, underground
burial chambers dating back 4,500 years that are one of the
prehistoric wonders of Spain. And next time we will take
a side trip on the loop road that goes to Carratraca, a spa
since Greek and Roman times that has been restored. And
I will bathe in the tub used by Empress Eugenie.

　　This time we slept in a nondescript hotel in Estepona,
then drove straight to Ronda. The old city gleamed white
on a white cliff like a mirage. The weather was crisp on the
high Serrania de Ronda, so off-season cold we saw only a
few tourists, not the summer hordes who have been troop-
ing to this romantic place of *bandaleros* and bullfights since
the nineteenth century.

　　We parked in the plaza and visited Spain's second
oldest bullring, an oval of ochre sand and warm stucco

walls. In the adjoining bullfight museum we fingered the
gold-filigreed capes and pantaloons of famous matadors —
men smaller than you'd expect, graceful as ballet dancers
but stringy and heartless as wolfhounds. After warming
up with a cup of thick coffee and a slug of cheap Spanish
brandy, we walked across the New Bridge (c. 1793) that
splits the old Moorish town from the newer Christian
Mercadillo section.

Once again I was walking in my own footsteps. Looking down 500 feet to the bottom of the precipitous limestone chasm of the Guadalevin River, I meditated on the
fate of Loyalists thrown off this bridge during the Civil
War. I remembered Dick Hugo wandering away from the
gorge to drink in workingmen's bars, rejoining us at dusk,
flushed and happy with wine. I remembered an angry old
gypsy woman who grabbed my coat and demanded pesos.
I remembered Dave talking about Ernest Hemingway,
who used Ronda as the setting of *For Whom the Bell
Tolls* — poor Dave, who wanted to be like Orson Wells,
making revolutionary movies and dancing in the streets
at the September *feria*.

That night Bill and I reposed in elegance at the
Edwardian-style Hotel Reina Victoria, built in 1906 to
house British railroad crews. Rilke stayed in room 208 during the winter of 1913, and his statue stands in the cliff-top
courtyard overlooking a crescent of fields and mountains
that shines blue in the mist. Next morning I posed Bill next
to Rilke. It was the same angle as a photograph Dave had
taken of Dick Hugo twenty-five years before.

c   c   c

Bill and I would have been content to stay in Ronda until spring, when the gardens around the walled city bloom. We could hike the gorge, see the caves at nearby La Pileta. I am told that a guide will equip you with old-fashioned gas headlamps and lead you into grottos where Paleolithic horses and goats grace the walls. Still further down in the deeps, you can shine your lanterns onto Neolithic stick-figures—art older than the famous works at Altamira. But we had a plane to catch in Paris the next week and miles to go, toward Madrid and the Pyrenees.

Driving west and south from Ronda we took a mountain road through chestnut groves and evergreen oaks to whitewashed Grazalema. The Serrania de Ronda is sprinkled with small Moorish hilltowns called *pueblos blancos,* and this one, more visited than most, is perhaps too pretty-perfect with its potted geraniums and narrow walled streets. Above the town is the entrance to the recently created Nature Park of Grazalema, a 116,000-acre region of jagged peaks, curving valleys, and pine-blanketed hillsides where you can camp, hike, or take horses into the green wild.

We headed north toward Las Palomas Pass, noting the locked entrance to a woodland preserve of *pinsapos,* a species of tall, pyramid-shaped pines found nowhere else in Europe. To enter the preserve you must get a permit from the provincial parks director in Cadiz, which we had not done, so we topped the pass in late-afternoon shadows and zigzagged down into Zahara.

Zahara is Arabian as its name, a stunning white village with roofs of red tile, window boxes filled with pink and magenta flowers even in January. Zahara has steep cobbled streets and is perched at the foot of an immense jutting rock. It is old. At the very top of the rock, like an eagle's nest, are ruins of a castle and an ancient tower built by Romans, restored by Arabs.

A Jeep Cherokee loaded with Americans stopped in front of the small hotel on the plaza. Bill and I watched the young people unload backpacks and duffels. They were suntanned, the men bearded, the women lean. We guessed they'd just come down from a mountain adventure.

Next time, we promised each other, we will come to the Serrania de Ronda in the Andalusian springtime. We will explore caves, ride horseback in the Sierra, hike through a forest of rare *pinsapos*. Andalusia is a place that can pierce your heart like memory. It is bare and basic as a widow veiled in black. It wails with the music of Arabs, dances the blood-sport of bulls and prancing cowboys, offers a vision of gardens in the desert no Nevada developer could ever dream.

In my fantasy of return, I come back to Zahara with Bill, maybe with my sons and their wives, my aging, laughing sisters. When the sun sets and the day cools, we will carry our bags into the only hotel on the plaza and sit on the balcony to eat *tapas* of *chorizo* and *morcilla*. We will remember our dead and praise our living as we drink the strong red wine.

The Importance of Dunes

Sumor. The Old English word tastes sweet, like peaches.
One dictionary definition says, "Any period regarded as a
time of fruition, fulfillment, happiness or beauty." This
pure and easy concept of summer is beguiling, but fraudu-
lent as nostalgia. I remind myself that summer's peach
must have at its heart a pit, a seed, the hint of bitterness.

All the summers of my childhood, I lived on the
beaches of Lake Michigan. My second-story bedroom faced
west, toward the lake. I slept with the sounds of waves lap-
ping or waves crashing, waves roaring in the gusts and
thunder of an electrical storm. There were gulls diving,
and thin-legged sandpipers on the beach where I stood.
When sky drops into lake and waves pull at your toes, any
summer child knows she is on the edge — a small person in
a great blue world.

The creatures who lived in the sand were also small
and sometimes stinging: sand fleas, burrowing wasps, red
ants, beetles, a swarm of ladybugs on my baby sister's bottom. I tried to catch minnows in the shallows where a
warm, urine-colored stream ran into the lake; my little sisters and I hopped after frogs and trapped tadpoles in jars so
we could watch their astounding tails turn into feet.
Alewives washed up on the beach some years, so many and
so rank that we would rake them into a pile a foot high, dig

a deep hole, and bury them to keep our beach from smelling of fishy death. We tried to catch the gold, black-veined monarch butterflies in nets, but I hated the powdery feel of their wings and the clumsiness of my fingers.

Once I witnessed the killing of a snake. My father's cousin, Paul, on furlough from World War II, had come to visit. He was slim, dark, romantic—the only soldier I knew. I was riding his back, playing horsey on the beach, when a curious movement where nothing should have moved froze him. A gray, diamond-marked twist of drift-wood had come alive at our feet.

"Rattlesnake," Paul screamed and dumped me in the sand. He grabbed a large stick and clubbed the snake to death. I was more scared of Paul's violence than I was of the snake.

After the war, Paul would give me his Purple Heart, but he had been wounded beyond any healing. He would change his name to Paul Armstrong (Hungarian Jew turned All-American Boy), ditch his European, educated ways and become a busboy in greasy spoons from Kansas City to Baton Rouge. He would descend into catatonia until scientists invented anti-psychotic drugs. Then he grew fat, lived in cheap hotels in Chicago, and peeped into windows at naked women. One evening he choked to death on a five-inch slab of steak. I never really knew Paul—except for our encounter with the snake. I like snakes.

⌐   ⌐   ⌐

The beaches where I discovered venom are on the south-eastern shores of the lake, past the refineries and steel mills of Gary, Indiana, some eighty miles east of Chicago. My family spent summers in the resort town of Lakeside, Michigan, until I was seven, then bought an unfinished house in a beach community called Tower Hill Shorelands near Warren Dunes State Park. My parents put in plumbing, paneled the walls with knotty pine, built a flagstone terrace. Fifty years later, when I visit my aged mother and father, I sleep in my old bedroom on the second floor, and waves still sing through the open French windows.

In Lakeside I learned to be ashamed of my body. My Hungarian parents had come to America from Paris, where I was born. French children played nude on the beaches; so did I. My parents were photographers. They liked to take pictures of me at the edge of waves — my plump legs, my little bucket. One hot July afternoon when I was two, a policeman accosted my father. "You better get that kid off our beach."

My father was perplexed.

"You're lucky I'm not pulling you in."

"But this is America!"

"You bet it's America. This is a Christian community."

The nuns in the convent adjoining the public beach had complained of my indecent exposure. I was rushed into panties, never again to feel unconscious in my body until I was grown and a mother and bathing in hot pools on the Middle Fork of the Salmon River, deep in the Idaho wilderness. Here is one value of wild places: You are not important there. You are a leaf, a common weed.

Life begins on a beach. Unlikely plants poke out of pure sand: marram grass, a razor-edged green pioneer waving to its followers — sea rocket, bugseed, winged pigweed, cocklebur. The beach is a desert, and that must be why, when I finally lived some months in the Sonoran

Desert, I felt drawn to it, happy in the spare, thorny
blossoming of life. Each cactus, yellow poppy, paloverde,
finger-leafed mesquite emerges as if newly created
from rocks turned sand. The Yaquis have a name for
their desert: the enchanted world of flowers.

Ancient creatures who emerged from waters to col-
onize beaches have left us legacies. My sisters and I often
walked on the lakeshore among green and rust-colored
pebbles, our backs stooped and aching, looking for fossils
we called Indian stones. These tiny round petrified worm-
animals with star-shaped holes were our jewels. My
mother, who knew little of geology but liked to make
stories, told me the fossils were a million years old. I
could barely comprehend one year. The Indian stones
strung around my neck signified time.

On clear August nights we girls would lie on our backs
on blankets, counting shooting stars. In Chicago, where
my family lived in an apartment through the long winter,
you could not see stars in the sky. It was luminous, smoky,
filled with the orange reflected light of the city. The beach
became our planetarium. We learned the names of constel-
lations. This was space.

You can fall in love with space and sky. A girl from
Chicago can go west and find mountains. These days I live
surrounded by grass on a high Montana meadow. There
is no water in sight, and yet the wind blows. The grass
undulates in sunshine. A hummingbird, iridescent, green
throated, plunges the needle of his tongue into a common
red petunia.

◧   ◧   ◧

The Importance of Dunes

Foredune. The word is a seduction. Prevailing winds blow sand inland until the particles hit an obstruction—a tuft of little blue-stem grass, a driftwood log. The grains pile up against the windward side of an object and, having lost their momentum, roll gently down the sheltered side, forming a mini-dune. In this sheltered space, sand cress, wild rye, bearberry, horsemint, hairy puccoon, even prickly pear cactus take hold. More sand accumulates, enriched by decaying vegetation and held secure by a network of tangled surface roots. Insects find sustenance, rodents burrow, songbirds fly from the oak forests to feast on seeds and berries. They are building a foredune.

The cliff at the edge of our beach is formed by waves of winter storms slicing into the foredunes. Severe winters cut the dunes back, leaving a wide, flat beach. Other years the water level rises, and the beach is a narrow walkway. The miniature mountains and cliffs rising from the beach to the more permanent tree-anchored dunes are my memory's password for play. When my sisters and I were water-logged, blue-lipped, and bored with swimming, we would leap from our cliff's tiered ledges. I was Wonder Woman with a beach-blanket cape.

Above the cliff, our no-man's-land of foredunes swelled to a wooded ridge. On top, where the sand turns smoky gray in the process of becoming dirt, our white frame house sits among oaks, pines, and sassafras trees, its wide screened-in porch looking west over the lake to the setting sun. On windy days, when it was too cold to swim, we sisters would descend the steep, splintery stairs from the house, cross a wooden ramp over the gully that separates foredunes from permanent dunes, and thread through thick, white-powdered poison ivy to the clearing where our cottonwood stood.

We nested in the tree and played house under its airy roof, collecting sand cherries and acorns for food, seed pods for money. A wind-borne cottonseed drifts to ground. Watered by rain, it may take hold. These trees grow fast, come to maturity, and begin to die within the span of a human life. I did not know that cottonwoods are the only trees that survive on foredunes. Ours was old in cotton-wood time.

Some days we carried a lunch of peanut-butter-and-jelly sandwiches, plums, chocolate-chip cookies, Kool-Aid in a thermos. Some days we brought dolls, a deck of Old Maid, our doctor's kit. We spread our blanket. We climbed the silver-limbed tree. The sun dove toward a purple horizon.

Clang, clang, our Grandma Beck beat on the horseshoe dinner bell. "Annick, Kaati, Carole — where are you?" She would call herself hoarse, with her Hungarian accent, but we would not answer. We were too busy playing doctor. Who can forget the probings of child-doctor hands? The unbearable tickle and tingle of a metal stethoscope on a bare nipple. Most little girls play doctor with boys and eventually we did, too, but awakening to sexuality in such female-child intimacy will for me always be linked to fore-dunes, tree-tops, soft green light, the rumble of white-capped waves. It is the domain of sisters.

While summering at Lakeside the year I turned seven, I became infected with polio, transmitted, perhaps, by other children on the swarming beach. At first it seemed another cold with sore throat, fever, exhaustion. "Just flu," said our country doctor, fishing in his black bag full of pink, purple, blue, yellow placebos. When I did not get better, my mother took me home to Chicago and our family physician. And then, in the middle of the night, I was bundled into blankets and rushed to Michael Reese Hospital, where another doctor put me through the pain of a spinal tap.

I was lucky; I did not become paralyzed. I fell ill at the apex of a great epidemic, before Jonas Salk discovered a vaccine. The children's polio ward was jammed with girls and boys, even babies, all of us together in a ballroom-sized infirmary. But even in the midst of my fright, I felt blessed. I was not, like the ten-year-old boy in the next bed, in an iron lung.

"Does it hurt?" I asked him.

"Not much."

"Are you scared?"

"Yes."

I remember wailing and nighttime moaning, swift nurses with white caps, and strong, white-jacketed orderlies who pushed wheelchairs and lifted the paralyzed children into insulting baby beds with slatted bars like playpens. I mostly observed and kept quiet and felt ashamed because I could move all my limbs. I played with the beautiful bride doll my parents had bought for me, and I read *Little Women, Lassie Come Home, The Wizard of Oz*. For the first time I felt truly alone. Myself.

It was the end of summer. I would come back to the beach more wary and yet more reckless. I would swim beyond the sandbar where the lake was cold and black at its bottom. My frantic mother would call me back, but I would keep swimming toward the horizon along the glittering path of the afternoon sun until my breath gave out. I had begun to learn no one is invulnerable. Take chances; you can be alone and not bored.

    ▣   ▣   ▣

Blowouts are sand craters, scooped out of the dunes by swirling winds. They are maybe fifty feet deep, flat and round at the bottom, fringed with jack pine and white pine on top, dotted with clumps of blue-leafed willow, starry false Solomon's seal, the ever-present marram grass.

You might come to a blowout with a serious novel, as I did with *Moby Dick,* and be lost in an ocean humming with whales. You might bring a sketch pad or try to write a poem. I would lie on my back and see faces in drifting clouds. The blowout was my place for dreaming, the inverse of mountains.

Occasionally my father would bring a model to the dunes to pose nude for arty photographs. We girls were not allowed to observe, but Kathy and I would sneak after them, the model in shorts, my father's neck strung with his Rolleiflex and lenses. They went in morning, when the light slanted and shadows were possible.

Creeping like the Potawatomi Indians who once walked a trail along the shore, we tracked the grown-ups to the blowout. The model would shed her bra and underpants. We held our breath. We had smelled the woman's perfume.

My father would direct the naked model toward the configuration of sand he wanted as background. He was also a sculptor, and he tried to capture an illusion of three-dimensions—a shaded thigh, breasts curving against the waves of sand. Voices drifted up to us, sometimes laughter. They never touched. Maybe my father knew we were spying. He was sexy—dark and handsome. We knew he loved women. We were in love with him, too. The blowout was a wild place where anything could happen.

It must have been tough for my mother—three

daughters, gorgeous models, all this adoration of her husband. No wonder she sometimes nagged and slammed doors, broke down in hysterical weeping, escaped to the beach for solace. I see her in my mind's eye striding away from us—a petite, pretty, buxom woman with good legs and a floppy hat.

I always thought of myself as my father's surrogate eldest son, and he was my main childhood hero. I would not learn to sew like my mother. I did not cook or bake my grandmother's fine Hungarian pastries. I cut my thick black hair short, wore jeans, knew the box scores of the Chicago Cubs, and preferred the company of men. And then, at eleven and a half, I was beseiged by hormones. I had not been paralyzed with polio, but as my body betrayed me into womanhood, I became paralyzed with self-consciousness. Awkward, slumped at the shoulders, withdrawn, I flinched from my father's embraces, not daring to shout the danger I felt: "Don't touch me!"

On the beach, in front of my parents and their friends, I took to shameless wrestling with a boy who lived down the road. I would drift far out into the lake with him, legs and arms entwined around a black inner-tube, exchanging wet kisses. I wonder what I was trying to prove. That I was free of my father? A girl sexy as any model? Normal? Wild?

Freedom from self-awareness came only when I was alone in the sand and grass, or reading, preferably both. That is why I loved the blowout, even the idea of the blowout, where I could think, feel, daydream, and meditate with no one watching but the beetles and crows. I was lucky to have found this haven so early and so close to hand. The peace I experienced in my blowout has shaped my life to a degree I could not have imagined in youth. I would grow up to be a solitary walker, like my mother, seeking solace in nature as others seek religion, booze, or drugs.

◻   ◻   ◻

Some anthropologists define and classify cultures by studying landscape patterns of habitation. One theory is called Prospect and Refuge, and I believe it applies to individuals as well as to cultures. The roots of such patterns can be traced to Stone Age hunters and gatherers and to the animals that were their models and their meat. Those who lived in the high open grasslands and savannas sought a dwelling place of prospect for predation and defense, like wolves, where they could spot herds of ungulates or invading tribes. Jungle peoples lived at the fecund bottom of life, looking up to monkeys in the trees, snakes curling like vines, the bright plumage of toucans.

But the places of greatest possibility and complexity—the places where higher cultures evolved—are at the edges of mountains and woods, looking down to a wider space. That is where our beach house sits, at the edge of an oak forest overlooking the lake. From childhood through adulthood, I have known artists and aspired to be one, and in my experience, artists (and western Indians) will choose prospect over refuge any day, unless they can have both.

Carl Sandburg once lived down our sandy road in Tower Hill. Just before we bought our place, he moved a few miles away to a farm in Harbert, where his wife raised goats. My father took us to visit, but Sandburg was not home. What I remember are the goats. Gregarious,

bearded creatures, they ambled on the sod-roofed house;
one jumped on the hood of our Buick.

The dunes have been a retreat for Chicago artists and
intellectuals since the early 1900s, and literary warriors
were our neighbors and visitors. Young Norman Maclean
would ride with Sherwood Anderson on what he called
the "Yellow Peril" (the electric train that ran from Chicago
to South Bend, Indiana) to visit his mentor, the historian
Ferdinand Schevill. Nelson Algren came to drink whiskey
on our porch, and we listened to his stories as the sun slid
into the lake. The Greek-American writer Harry Petrakis,
another friend, still lives near New Buffalo. Ben Burns,
who edited *The Chicago Defender* in the 1940s and was
managing editor of *Ebony,* has remodeled Sandburg's old
studio into a spacious house. When he moved to North
Carolina at age sixty-seven, Sandburg said, "It's only my
ghost that's leaving the Middle West."

☐　☐　☐

The dunes are full of ghosts. The oldest are prehistoric
mammoths, mastodons, giant beaver. Retreating glaciers
carved the Great Lakes, and our geologically young dunes
blow up against moraines, drifts, and outwash plains.
Under the sand are the limestone beds of a Paleozoic sea,
piled up over millions of years before the coming of verte-
brate life. Sand upon sand upon sand is a way I like to
think about history.

In ancient times, B.C. 100 to A.D. 700, Hopewell Indians
established villages and summer gardens near New Buffalo.
A few miles inland from our beach, near the town of Three
Oaks, they dug pits to store corn, wild rice, beans, and

root crops. My family went to Three Oaks for fresh food—
sweet corn and ripe tomatoes at roadside stands. We
filled coffee cans with blueberries off the bush and picked
bushels of golden delicious apples from the orchards.

A forest band of Potawatomi lived near St. Joseph,
Michigan, where my Old-Country grandmothers would go
to "take the waters," easing their rheumatic limbs into the
mineral baths of a Victorian spa. In 1838 the Potawatomi,
casualties of white man's measles and small pox and white
man's wars, were packed off to a reservation in Oklahoma.
One recalcitrant band moved to Cass County, Michigan,
where a small group still lives. I identify with survivors;
many of my relatives died in Auschwitz.

Much of the thronging wildlife that lived by the lake
did not survive. Bison were hunted out by Indians and
whites by 1750. Even before white settlement began, during the trapper's era in the early 1800s, elk and most of the
beaver had been killed off. Timber wolves were extermi-
nated a few years before most of the deer were shot in 1873,
which is when the last wild turkey graced a pioneer's table.
Before long there were no more black bears, panthers, lynx,
otters, or wolverines. And in 1880 the last flocks of passen-
ger pigeons darkened the skies over our dunes.

Wild ducks and geese used to fly over the lake in great
Vs when I was a child. Now there are only a few small
flocks. Huge sturgeon once swam up local streams in the
spring spawning run. Farmers netted suckers by the wagon
load to be fed to hogs. At New Buffalo, fishermen caught
5,000 whitefish in one day. All this rich life is gone, but the
deer are coming back. For years I searched for deer among
the white oaks, red oaks, black oaks, dogwood, sassafras,
and basswood in our patch of forest. I tracked old game
trails but never saw even hoofprints. Until just last year, in

November, when I was amazed to see a fat mule deer racing across our beach at dawn. Deer, like rats and coyotes, are also survivors.

The legendary forests that spread to the east—Galien beeches, maples, and the famous "oak openings" that James Fenimore Cooper described—live only in the imaginations of readers like me. Lucky for my soul, it is still possible to glimpse a sight of the aboriginal woods in the nature sanctuary of Warren Woods, near Lakeside. I remember taking Sunday visitors to walk among the giant beeches, the woods hushed and filled with sunlight at their tops, cool in midsummer along the green-shaded paths. Those walks were as close as I had come in childhood to what church is supposed to be.

The forest behind our house at Tower Hill is a spiritual retreat, under covenant never to be developed further. I could not know firsthand the primeval deep woods of Michigan, but ours is filled with pussytoes, asters, and bastard toadflax. With my mother and sisters I gathered wild geraniums in June, blue and yellow violets in May. Best of all was April, when trees had not yet come into leaf but the delicate, white, orchid-centered trilliums lit the earth in the aftermath of a spring snow.

I love to return to Tower Hill in early spring when our woods are ethereal, filled with a dank perfume from layers of rotting leaves, hushed except for the raucous bluejays that hunt eggs in the nests of red, crested cardinals. These are my family's sacred groves. The only people who live on the other side of the road are a handful of vacationing ministers. We understand each other. We pray in our ways to the god of the deep woods.

E   E   E

The moving dunes in the state park down the beach from our summer house change shape from season to season. My sisters and I have come to maturity transformed and transforming like dunes that won't stay put. We who still think of ourselves as children have children old enough to be mothers and fathers. Very little remains the same except for Old Baldy, the highest dune, which we climbed as if it were Mount Everest.

It would be an expedition, with rucksacks full of snacks and towels. Kathy, Carole, and I and several neighbor kids would parade past the church camp to the public beach where bathers of all shapes, ages, and colors camped under red-striped umbrellas. Old Baldy loomed above the stove-hot cement of the parking lot, its steep flank hollowed like the trough of a wave. We'd race to the top, drop our loads, and somersault down. We landed laughing, our mouths filled with sand.

Anchoring the sloping backside of our mountain were thick stands of pine, poplars, and poison ivy. We swung on vines—"Me Tarzan, you Jane"—and the littlest kids had to be chimps. Behind Old Baldy the dunes spread like the Sahara. In moonlight, when I was seventeen and in love with a fair-haired Minnesota boy named David Smith, the great dune was our necking tryst. Once, rolling and panting at the edge of the woods, I forgot about poison ivy. The next week in high school, the gym teacher would not let me into the swimming pool with my crusty, oozing sores. I learned that love is full of perils. A year later, lying on sand, Dave said: "I love your mind, your soul, your body." What more could a girl ask?

I married Dave Smith when I was nineteen. After he graduated from law school at the University of Chicago, we made our escape from the Midwest with six-month-old

Eric. My trajectory from that time to now has been west-
ward and upward, toward the last wild places, toward
those who would share with me the ecstatic pull of landscape and sky. On the homestead Dave and I built in western Montana, I am surrounded by meadows. Bear and elk
roam in my woods, and coyotes howl from the deep grass.
Desire for wildness is what I took from the beach, the foredunes, the blowout.

     C   C   C

Think of a funnel. The Michigan dunes have been a gathering place for four generations blown in from Hungary and
France and Montana, from Chicago, Boston, California,
and Texas. Dave and I bore four children who would learn
to walk with us on sand. My sisters also married and had
babies. For twenty-five years the eight cousins have spent
summer days on our beach, bringing sweethearts now,
spouses, and my mother's first great-grandchild.

Our family album is filled with elongating limbs and
silvering hair — playing, like these memories, against the
blues and browns of lake and sand. Some faces are gone:
Dave, dead in 1974; Kathy's husband, Chris, dead in 1976;
Nelson Algren, dead in 1981. My parents are coming
ninety. I shudder to think who will be the next ghost.

The dunes are changing with us: more summer
mansions; retaining walls to keep the dunes from eroding;
our blowout filled in by a Caterpillar bulldozer for a resort
development. Accustomed to Montana mountains, I see
Old Baldy small as an anthill. Perhaps it has joined the
ranks of the aging, the shrinking. Hang gliders fly around
the big dune's pine-fringed pate; windsurfers slalom off-
shore. Four miles down the beach at Bridgman, where

terrorist Wobblies once hid from the law, we stare at the ominous cone of a nuclear power plant. Lake waters cool its reactors.

Winter and summer since my father retired, my parents spend most of their days at the dunes. He sculpted nudes from hardwood until arthritis in both shoulders made him stop. Now he watches birds, listens to music, and reads. She cooks, sews, walks the beach as always. Mother is in love with generation. She wants to hold a mob of great-grandchildren in her arms. We know winter is coming, the wildest season. Waves will freeze in mid-motion. Snow will make lace of the woods. Spindrift will meld with sand. Winter will be heavy and elusive as mercury.

Not long ago, my sister Kathy and I came to the dunes in winter. We walked the beach with Mother. She is small as a child these days, yet strong on her still good-looking legs. She rushed ahead of us in a stinging wind. We were walking the frozen foam when we saw her tumble head-long into a patch of deep slush. We pulled her out, wet to the waist and giggling. We held her and dried her—our daughter.

I have come back to the edge, where water and sand create unlikely life. There are snakes in the marram grass, and monarch butterflies so rare we don't dare catch them, and Indian stones from Paleozoic seas. After fifty years of watching, I have seen one sleek doe race across our beach, and I shouted for the pure surprising joy of the deer's return. The dunes are moving. The dance is monotonous, evanescent and shifting . . . one-step, one-step, one-step. It is my heart. I am summer's white-haired child in love with this blue world.

Notes

Portions of this book have appeared in the following publications:

A briefer version of "Homestead" was published in *Montana Spaces*, ed. William Kittredge (New York: Nick Lyons Press, 1988).

"Better than Myth" is derived from the introduction to part 3 of *The Last Best Place: A Montana Anthology*, ed. William Kittredge and Annick Smith (Helena: Montana Historical Society Press, 1988.)

"Law of the Range" is based on my introduction, "What You See Is What You Got," to *Law of the Range: Portraits of Old-Time Brand Inspectors*, by Stephen Collector (Livingston, Montana: Clark City Press, 1991).

Portions of "The River That Runs Through It" appeared in an essay of the same name in *Big Sky Journal* (Summer 1994) and in "The Blackfoot Years," *Outside* (April 1990).

A briefer version of "The Rites of Snow" was published in *Outside* (January 1993).

The first section of "Country and Western" is derived from "Big Sky Mudflaps," *Rocky Mountain Magazine* (May/June 1980).

"In the Garden with Beasts" was published as "Camping in Montana," *New Choices* (May 1991).

A briefer version of "Ride" began as "The Greenhorn Trail," *Outside* (August 1993).

"Wallowa" is based on "Renegade Spirits on Highway 3," published in *Outside* (August 1991).

"Fishing the Tundra" was published in *Travel and Leisure* (March 1994).

Portions of "Andalusia, Again" appeared in "Rolling to Ronda," *Outside* (March 1994).

"The Importance of Dunes" was published in *Outside* (August 1994).

The following material is quoted in this book:

Meriwether Lewis and William Clark, *Journals of Lewis and Clark* (New York: Heritage Press, 1962).

Czeslaw Milosz, *Beginning with My Streets: Essays and Recollections* (New York: Farrar, Strauss, & Giroux, 1992).

E. C. Abbott, *We Pointed Them North: Recollections of a Cowpuncher* (Norman: University of Oklahoma Press, 1976).

Granville Stuart, *Forty Years on the Frontier* (Cleveland: Arthur H. Clark, 1925).

Frank Linderman, *Plenty-Coups, Chief of the Crows* (Lincoln: University of Nebraska Press, 1962).

Mary Ronan, *Frontier Woman: The Story of Mary Ronan as Told to Margaret Ronan*, ed. H. G. Merriam (Missoula: University of Montana Press, 1973).

Thomas J. Dimsdale, *Vigilantes of Montana* (Norman: University of Oklahoma Press, 1977).

Elizabeth Custer, *Boots and Saddles, or, Life in Dakota with General Custer* (New York: Harper and Brothers, 1902).

James Willard Schultz, *My Life as an Indian* (Williamstown, Mass.: Corner House, 1974).

Chief Charlot, "The Indian and Taxation," in *The Last Best Place: A Montana Anthology,* ed. William Kittridge and Annick Smith (Helena: Montana Historical Society Press, 1988).

Charles M. Russell, "The Story of a Cowpuncher," in *Trails Plowed Under* (New York: Doubleday, 1927).

L. A. Huffman quote can be found in Mark H. Brown and W. R. Felton, *Before Barbed Wire* (New York: Bramhall House, 1956).

Notes

Edward S. Curtis, *The North American Indian* (New York: Johnson Reprint Co., 1970).

Norman Maclean, *A River Runs Through It* (Chicago: University of Chicago Press, 1979).

The lines from Richard Hugo's poems "The Milltown Union Bar," "The Only Bar in Dixon," and "My Buddy" are reprinted from *Making Certain It Goes On: The Collected Poems of Richard Hugo* by permission of W. W. Norton and Company, Inc. Copyright © 1984 by the Estate of Richard Hugo.

"Rainbow At Midnight." Words and music by "Lost" John Miller. Copyright © 1946 Shapiro, Bernstein & Co., Inc., New York. Copyright renewed. International copyright secured. All rights reserved. Used by permission.

Rainer Maria Rilke, *The Sonnets to Orpheus,* trans. Stephen Mitchell (New York: Touchstone, 1986).

Annick Smith is a writer of essays and short fiction and a filmmaker whose feature film credits include *A River Runs Through It* and *Heartland*. She was coeditor with William Kittredge of *The Last Best Place: A Montana Anthology,* and is currently writing a book about the tallgrass prairie in Oklahoma's Osage Hills. Born in Paris, raised in Chicago, Smith is a widow who has lived for twenty-five years on the homestead ranch in western Montana where she raised her four sons.

This book is part of LITERATURE FOR A LAND ETHIC, a Milkweed Editions program that presents literature as an important voice to explore, educate, promote dialogue, and foster action on the critical environmental issues of our communities.

Milkweed Editions publishes with the intention of making a humane impact on society, in the belief that literature is a transformative art uniquely able to convey the essential experiences of the human heart and spirit.

To that end, Milkweed Editions publishes distinctive voices of literary merit in handsomely designed, visually dynamic books, exploring the ethical, cultural, and esthetic issues that free societies need continually to address.

Milkweed Editions is a not-for-profit press.